MW00973654

Eight Months

This Is
Not Going
To Work

JOHN VALDEZ

ALLIPSA MEDIA

An imprint of Parkwood West Management, Inc.
allipsa.com

Copyright © 2017 Allipsa Media
First Edition
First Printing

All rights reserved. No portion of this book may be reproduced, stored in a retrieval system, or transmitted in any form or by any means—electronic, mechanical, photocopy, recording, scanning, or any other—except for brief quotations in critical reviews or articles, without the prior written permission of the publisher.

Quotes from the *JESUS* film closing script are used by permission. *JESUS*, © 1979 - 2017, Inspirational Films, Inc. All rights reserved. No unauthorized duplication, reproduction, distribution, broadcast or exhibition without written permission. www.JesusFilmStore.com

Scripture quotations in The Jesus Video Project are from The Good News Translation (GNT), Copyright © 1976 by the American Bible Society (ABS). Used by Permission.

All other scripture references from the Holy Bible, NEW INTERNATIONAL VERSION®, NIV® Copyright © 1973, 1978, 1984, 2011 by Biblica, Inc.® Used by permission. All rights reserved worldwide.

Cover by Katie: Leucadia life. Author & the kids in earlier days.

ISBN: 0-9989225-0-1.
ISBN-13: 978-0-9989225-0-8

DEDICATION

To Miss Meyerhoff, my 9th grade English teacher. On the last day of class, you made me promise to write you a story some day. Well, here it is. In fact, here are several. I'm sorry to be handing this in so late.

To Alice Ricciardi, barista at Caffè del Doge. Not long ago I was adrift in Venice, scribbling notes in your caffè, and you asked if I was an author. I doubt you remember, but at that moment, you inspired me to say yes, and to finalize and publish *Eight Months*.

CONTENTS

EXPLICIT CHRISTIAN CONTENT

"POEYMS, PLATITUDES & a PLAY"

POEYMS

PLATITUDES

… & a PLAY

BETWEEN YOU AND ME

One million years ago, when I first wrote many of these stories for The Coast News, I styled them so that they would "hold up" over time. At some point, perhaps a half-million years ago, I assembled the stories, added a few more, and made a book manuscript, which I sent to one (1) publisher's purgatory pile. Unsurprisingly, it was rejected. I threw the manuscript into an old cabinet and got on with my life.

I came back to it not long ago and literally dusted it off. At first, I was tempted to rewrite the thing to reflect the effects of modern technology. But I decided not to when, to my surprise, younger people begged me to leave it alone in order to show what life was like a million years ago. Also, since the stories had held up very well, there was no need to force tech updates into the manuscript to make it seem "contemporary." That would make it out of date by tomorrow, anyway.

Now, as an over a million-year-old, I've recognized I better put it out there. I've finally realized that at some point in life, I gotta do what I'm here to do.

So I combed out the minor errors that I'd left for the hoped-for "publisher," trimmed it a little here, punched it up a little there, and present it to you now, somewhat vintage and in mint condition. She's an old gal, but a perennial classic. I hope you enjoy.

As I write this, three houses nearby are being demolished for McMansions. Those of us who would "Keep Leucadia Funky" are losing the battle. Gentrification is upon us, so I invite you to treasure these tales, written in a time and a world that is quickly slipping away.

John Valdez
May, 2017
Leucadia, California

ACKNOWLEDGMENTS

Thank you to my **wonderful wife and family**, both for your inspiration and for your long-suffering with this project in particular, and with me in general. Those of you with writers in the family will understand.

Thank you to the world's best editor, **Jim Kydd**, Editor of The Coast News, who got me started, and who lets his writers write. Thanks to **Nynah Mckenzie** at Coffee-Coffee, a ray of sunshine and a born encourager, for your unconditional support and enthusiasm which helped me get through the part when I thought I'd never finish.

Thanks to the entire "**crew at Cru**" for guiding me through permissions. Your helpfulness, encouragement and professionalism made it an enjoyable process, and you went above and beyond to help me make *Eight Months* even better than it otherwise would have been.

Thank you to my barber, **Gino Grygera**. Every six weeks I sat in your chair and told you this book would absolutely be ready "the next time I see you." I finally instructed you to stab me in the neck with your scissors if the publication date slipped any further, and when it did, you didn't. I'm grateful for the motivation, and the mercy.

Thank you to **Dillan Stockham**, of Stockham Media, for the invaluable media graphics tech help. You rescued me.

I thank my wife and the other advance readers: **Janet and Bruce Adams, Barb & Alan Amavisca, Ray Daily, Brian Douglas, Michelle Gunnell Glenn, Danielle Leopold and Jodi Smith** for telling me when it was working, when it wasn't working, and when to stop working and just publish this thing.

Eight
Months

JANUARY

Tuesday.

It's Tuesday and I'm free. I stretch, rub my face and check the time. It's 9:54 a.m. Wow. 9:54, already? I slept for … nearly … fourteen hours. I sit on the edge of the bed. I'm free.

Yesterday, I quit. I walked in and I quit my job. I quit corporate life.

My career in corporate life began twenty years ago, as a fresh-faced business school graduate, eager to show the world how much I knew and how much I could do. I had chosen the small but prestigious CPA firm of Brotman, Brotman & Young, largely because of "The Jerry Brotman Effect." Jerry Brotman was a well-known local personality, bon vivant, and legendary business tycoon. As a wonder-boy wannabe, I hoped that by joining Jerry's firm I would learn from and share my insights with Jerry, the wonder-boy extraordinaire.

I had taken extra classes during college in order to finish quickly and had graduated Magna Cum Laude. I was an inquisitive and philosophical student, always sitting in the front row and initiating thought-provoking discussions with my professors on the fine points of the subject at hand. At least, *I* thought the discussions were thought-provoking, but on more than one occasion one of my fellow students approached me after class to say, "I have no idea what you two were talking about." I had yet to learn that the world wouldn't generally pay much for thought-provoking discussions on the fine points of the subject at hand.

My first job performance review set the tone for all of my years in corporate life that followed. I remember the honking of car horns and the sounds of a siren welling up from the street eight floors below to my cubicle, where I labored on an adding machine, wearing my best suit, waiting to discuss my progress, strengths, (and, if applicable, weaknesses) that had become evident during the ninety days I had served Mr. Brotman.

I'd been waiting all afternoon and now it was near the end of the day. Mr. Brotman's secretary finally led me to his office and instructed me to wait.

I looked around Mr. Brotman's impressive corner office. The south window looked down on the Civic Center with its modern concrete parking structure and beyond to downtown. The west window was filled with a sweeping view across San Diego Bay, to the Coronado Strand and the vast blue Pacific beyond.

I turned to study the memorabilia on the other two walls. The office was essentially an elaborate and impressive shrine to Jerry Brotman: A picture of Brotman shaking hands with the President of the United States of America, a dead and exotic animal head, a picture of Brotman in Africa kneeling next to said crumpled exotic dead animal while it still had its head. The distant dead eyes, fogged over in the picture, had been replaced by lively glass eyes. There were various framed Declarations, such as the one from the Office of the Mayor, declaring as best I could interpret it, that "Whereas Brotman, having worked tirelessly to promote the general well being and good standing of ... Brotman, and whereas Brotman, having ... (essentially crossed) Official (palms in maybe not such official ways), and whereas Brotman did (this and that, and the other and such, and so very much), Now Therefore, be it herein resolved, that by unanimous Decree (such and such a) Date shall now and forever be known as Jerry Brotman Day."

I stood dutifully admiring a picture of Brotman shaking some bald guy's hand while standing on home plate, presenting a beach blanket sized check with two commas in it, when Brotman himself strode brusquely into his office, went over to his desk, and sat down. As he did, I noticed that over Brotman's left shoulder there was a man standing on the concrete ledge of the parking garage next door. He was in his mid-30's, and had messy, sandy-blond hair, and wore jeans, a t-shirt and white socks.

The sirens grew louder.

He was going to kill himself. During my job performance review. My first job review in my first job out of college.

Maybe not *kill* himself. The parking structure, like most, had low ceilings and although he was five levels up, he really wasn't very high off the ground. And there were bushes below him. If he jumped, he might only succeed in making a real mess of himself. I presume he was fed up and wanted to end the grip of failure on his life. How pitiful if he should fail even in his plan to stop failing.

I wanted him to live. I wanted him to step back from the edge, to breathe the air of this planet, to feel forgiven by himself and others and by God, who I prayed would show this man a better way of breaking the grip of failure in his life.

Years before I had written out a small treatise about life, sort of my own personal Desiderata. If I could have reached that man and brought him down from that ledge, and taken him somewhere restful and given him a good meal and let him recover from all that had traumatized him, if I could have rescued him from himself, I would have read him my little treatise:

Imagine all of the matter in the universe. Imagine all of the distance between that matter. It's incomprehensible.

How much of all that exists, has ever contained that which we call, "life"?

All of the known life in the universe exists on the skin of one planet. If it occurs again in the universe, it does not do so for an incomprehensible distance. Life is so rare.

And at this moment, the space in the universe that you occupy is filled with life. Your life. Your one life.

If you have life, you exist, and you can know that you exist. Life is the celebration, of the realization, of Being.

This is the reason I cannot pity you.

John Valdez

But I couldn't reach him and I couldn't rescue him. He stood on the ledge of the parking garage while his life and my career, or at least my job review, hung in the balance. It is terrifying and upsetting to see another human life in peril, on the brink of death.

I said to Mr. Brotman, "Perhaps this isn't the best time for us to conduct my job performance review."

"Why not?" he demanded.

I pointed over his left shoulder. Brotman wheeled around to look out the window at the man, teetering, in his socks, on the edge, his shoes neatly paired next to him on the ledge. I mumbled something about the life of a fellow human being in the balance. He said, "Sheesh!!" and whisked the curtains shut, then turned back around to me. Then he leaned over his desk and said, "Never mind him. We need to talk about your speed on the adding machine. Mr. Valdez, you need to *become the machine.*"

In the months that followed that first job review, I endeavored to become the machine, just as Jerry demanded. I was determined to get on top of this job and impress Jerry so that someday maybe we could go quail hunting together or something.

Of course it seemed unfair that Brotman had the right to live large while I was expected to "become the machine." But with enough hard work and dedication, the day would come when I could stop being the machine and start shooting animals in Africa and schmoozing politicians and have a Day officially declared for me, when I could turn to underlings like me and tell them to "become the machine" in order to provide for my lavish lifestyle.

Brotman was one of those rare guys who got a double portion on God's assembly line and I am certain whoever was in line behind him got no brains at all. Until I met Brotman, I had always thought the people who lived large were necessarily terrible at details and paperwork. But Brotman could charm and guffaw and slap backs and hold his liquor and shoot animals like Hemingway, yet *still* master the nuances of the most complicated Tax Codes and breeze through paperwork as though it were child's play, whereas Mr. Hemingway, I understand, occasionally forgot to file any tax forms at all.

Brotman appeared one day while we were slaving to complete the audit of one of our clients, a hotel chain owned by one Milton Weinstein.

Brotman produced an adding machine and sat down to a mountain of reports, each one containing page after page of worksheets, each worksheet containing column after column of numbers. Brotman could somehow intuitively go to exactly the right report, worksheet, page, column and number that he wanted to extract, all the while firing questions in rapid fire succession at the audit supervisors, my bosses:

"Mark, have you tied in the depreciation schedule to the asset list? Rose, is there any funny stuff buried in office expense? Jeff, why aren't they using the same inventory system for tax and book?" Mark, Rose, and Jeff answered all at once. Meanwhile, he had extracted Mark's depreciation schedule from the stack of papers and rechecked the figures on his adding machine, his fingers a blur. He listened to all the answers at once while digging into Jeff about the inventory system: "Tell them they're wasting money and to set them both up the same way," while Rose kept talking. By then he had his hands on the office expense numbers and said to Rose, "Tell Milt you need the backup on this item here, here and this one here. Wait until I leave. Mark, your schedule looks fine." Then he pulled out a list and dumped about three days of work on us, which for me would take about five. He stood up, snapped his briefcase closed, and went off to schmooze with Milt, while making him feel fabulous about paying us a lot of money to stick our noses into his business. We heard them cackling and belly-laughing from all the way down the hall. He had been in the building fifteen minutes. The Jerry Brotman Effect.

I was, and ever will be, far inferior to Brotman at both "living large" and "being the machine." Brotman was impossible to dislike when he chose to be charming, and had fine, handsome features and a full head of hair. Six hours of sleep was too much for him, and though he was twenty years my senior, he was in far better physical shape than I. He emanated a radiance and vitality that instantly melted women, yet he was a gentleman. His personal life was distinguished by four kids, one wife, and no rumors.

He was brilliant and articulate and had friends everywhere, so everybody had to either like him or had to pretend to like him. When I was around Jerry I always felt like I must have been the guy right behind him in God's assembly line, the guy who didn't get much of anything.

Though I was intimidated, I couldn't be jealous. Jerry had worked very hard to achieve everything he had. He had done what one must do to get where he was, and I respected that.

During one of Jerry's later appearances, I had the bad fortune of Jerry extracting one of *my* worksheets from the stack. My printing was terrible and my worksheets were frankly hideous and frightening to look upon. They consisted of long, wavering columns of individually crafted numbers, each figure a carefully written and unique creation, like a snowflake. These laboriously assembled worksheets took me hours and hours to compile with nervous, unsteady hands. The longer I labored, the more my confidence in myself and the confidence of my supervisors etched away, and the slower and klutzier I got.

Jerry held up my worksheet and dangled it by the corner, tweezered between thumb and forefinger, his mouth turned down as though the paper stunk, his head shaking. He mumbled, "Check this, Rose," handed it to her, and left, less than pleased.

Jerry, the big boss, was onto me, and the appearance of my work became worse and worse as I grew more and more self-conscious and tense about how it looked. The problem wasn't carelessness or sloppiness—it was panic. My printing was way over micromanaged and tense. I gritted my teeth and worked harder and harder and began to burn myself out which, I felt, was worth it because as soon as I got over the top I would be able to shift into a higher gear and move up and along in my career.

But my crummy-looking handwriting had put my work under more scrutiny and one afternoon as I was flailing away, trying to keep up and catch up and be the machine and get ahead, Rose walked in holding one of my worksheets by the corner. Her nose was wrinkled up and her mouth was turned down as though the paper stunk.

She had found three or four errors on the sheet, which I couldn't explain except to say, "I guess I messed up." These errors meant that the whole sheet was wrong, so all the totals were wrong. Other people had used those wrong totals in their work which meant that everyone who was working on the project would have to stop until the whole worksheet could be redone.

I reached out to take the worksheet from Rose so I could correct it, but she pulled it in, said, "No, I'll redo it," spun around and walked off. I knew right then that I was not going to go quail hunting with Mr. Jerry Brotman any time soon, or any time ever, and that the brightest moment I could look forward to in my future with Brotman, Brotman & Young would be a decent severance check.

That day came not long afterwards and Jerry again leaned over his desk, as he had done during my job performance review, glared at me and bellowed, "You should have *become the machine!*"

In the twenty years that followed, I tried my best to become the machine. I worked as hard and as long as I could in various companies and careers, and after many years of very hard work, ludicrous hours and countless thousands of miles on the road, built a career in Corporate Real Estate Development at a major national retail chain, which will remain nameless, to protect the guilty.

That was, until yesterday, when I went in and quit.

Maybe "quit" isn't the right word. Maybe "escaped" is better. An office building is a beautiful, nicely landscaped minimum-security prison, in that, if you have to be there, then you have to *be* there. You can step outside once in a while, but you can't really leave. You can't just say, "I am going to leave," and leave.

At best, its occupants are held by the invisible force fields of their own ambition, their expectation of personal, professional and corporate progress, and by the satisfaction of taking responsibility for and providing for the needs of family and self. More commonly, though, the sequestered souls in office buildings are bound by financial need, overspending, debt, and simple habit. Regardless, the same rule applies to both. You can't just leave, you have to escape, or—more often—transfer to another penitentiary. You are a prisoner, of sorts.

Jeannie escaped in an ambulance. Jeannie was a secretary at one of the companies I've worked for, and was under so much work stress that one afternoon her body locked up and she couldn't move or talk, so they called an ambulance and she went off and never came back. After that, some of the people in the office rather unkindly referred to her as, "Jeannie The Nut."

A few years ago, at another company, when I had just instructed our company cashier to wire transfer several hundred thousand dollars to complete the purchase of a real estate lease, I received a frantic call from our attorney: "John," he said, "I hope you haven't wired the money yet.

We got a big problem…" I got off the phone and ran as fast as I could down the hall to the cashier's office at the far end of the building. Unlike a check, which can have a "stop payment" put on it, with a wire transfer the moment the cashier pushes the button to wire the money, the money is gone, irretrievable. I reached the cashier just a few seconds before she pushed that button, stopped her in time, and breathed a big sigh of relief.

I had run past Donna, my boss, who was chatting near the hall with some friends. She stamped into the cashier's office.

"Wow, that was close," I told her. "The attorney just called to put a stop to the deal, and we were just about to wire the money." I expected her to say, "What's wrong with the deal?" or "Boy, it's a good thing you stopped the cashier on time."

Instead, she said, "I'm recommending that Claire (the Head of Human Resources) write you up for running in the building."

I smiled, enjoying her joke. "That's funny."

"Oh, no. I don't think you understand how serious it is when you run in the office. Someone could have been hurt. You know, John, if you get more than two write-ups, you're terminated."

She wasn't joking.

I said, "I just saved us a half a million bucks."

She rolled her eyes and let out a big sigh, then shook her permed head and wagged her manicured finger at me. "I don't know about that. Don't be insolent."

The more I tried to communicate, the clearer it was to her that I didn't understand the seriousness of my offense. What it boiled down to, was that I could see the error of my ways and apologize for it, or I could be "written up." Katie and I had a baby on the way. I apologized, acknowledging and expressing remorse for the danger I had put others in by running down the hall. She needed to hear these words, and once she did, she turned and strode happily back to her friends, never acknowledging that I had saved the company a half million on the wire transfer, not to mention a multi-million dollar lease that we would have been obligated to for a decade.

I will not miss that sort of thing in corporate life.

✳✳✳✳✳

Tuesday.

It's Tuesday and I'm free.

Last year at this time, I was back East at the Annual Meeting at Corporate Headquarters. Marvin Green, Chairman of the Board and Chief Executive Officer, stood at the podium and addressed we hundred or so Corporate Real Estate Acquisitions Executives. He lowered his head into his neck and cast a conspiratorial gaze about the room.

Locking eyes with we devoted executives through a bloodshot, bleary gaze, his voice rose then became shrill as he proclaimed, "This year, we have signed deals to open 400 new stores. We will open 500 new stores next year, and..." he paused, drowned out by delirious, sycophantic applause...

We understood what this meant: With this kind of growth, we would earn bonuses amounting, on average, to twice our already fat annual salaries. Four hundred stores in a year meant opening more than a store a day. Not to be a spoilsport, but I didn't get the feeling our store operations people were doing a very good job of running the stores that they already had. I knew what would happen if I dared to mention that observation to my boss, Roy Prince: "That isn't our problem," he would say. "That's an Operations problem. We just need to make deals to open the number of stores Marvin wants." I also knew what Roy would think: "Strike-mark against Valdez for questioning our strategic plan." If the corporate ship ever began to sink, I wanted to be as high above the waterline as possible, so it wasn't worth it to bring up the illogic of our growth plan.

...as the applause died down, our Corporate Emperor's skull hunkered even further down into his neck.

Suddenly, he slammed his forearms onto the top of the podium, lurched over it, and from deep inside his chest, proclaimed, "...the year after next, we will open SIX HUNDRED NEW STORES!" We exploded into obedient revelry, but it was obvious to me that it would be obvious to a child that this over-ambitious plan would someday leave Emperor Green with no clothes.

Yesterday, Monday morning, I came into work early, put my belongings into a cardboard box, and sat in my office, lights out, waiting for Roy to arrive. I heard him open his office door and turn on his lights. I heard the sound of him settling into his chair. I walked into his office. He looked up. I said, "I have decided to leave the Company." He looked at me, with surprise, then swung his chair and gazed out the window and said, "Okay..." Then, "Why?"

"I've sold a piece of property I own and have enough money for a year or more. My kids are growing up, and I am missing it. I want to spend a year with my family while I am still young. I don't want to wait until I am a grandfather to appreciate my family."

"Doesn't sound very responsible, financially, to sell real estate and live off of it."

"It isn't."

He gave me a curious look, as though wondering if there were more about this decision that I wasn't telling.

There was no need for me to mention that he was driving me crazy. I did not mention the twitch that had developed in my right eye. I did not mention that I had gone out to get some socks from the dryer while getting ready for work the other morning and my legs locked up and my body wouldn't move and I was afraid I was just days away from escaping in an ambulance like "Jeannie The Nut."

I also did not mention what we both knew—that the company's losses from operations were running at the rate of a hundred million dollars a month and the cash we were spending to open new stores would be sorely needed to keep our existing stores in business and that it was a matter of time before our so-called "growth" plan would come crashing down—that there would never be any bonuses paid when the company cancelled every deal we had put together over the last year.

That was incidental. I was ready to leave anyway.

I watched his jaw clench and release, clench and release, like Norman Bates upon being shown the guest register, as the slanted early morning light shone through the window and highlighted his angular face. Then he swung the chair back, looked straight at me and said, "I envy you. I … I could retire, I suppose. I've done well enough that I could probably afford to do it. I've thought about it, but I just don't know what I would *do* if I didn't have to come to work here every day. Besides, if I stay, I might be able to retire as a Vice President."

Roy and I spent Monday morning tying up loose ends. By noon, we shook hands and I walked out the door a free man. I got to leave. He had to stay. I left Roy to carry on until some future time when he would be consumed with fending off the sharks, protecting himself and his career while clinging to the scattered flotsam of a sinking corporate ship. In a way, my departure lightened the load and raised him slightly higher above the water line. He stood at the curb and waived as I pulled out, knowing that he dare not take the six-inch step off the concrete, lest he taste the air of freedom and leave everything, for ever, burning all bridges, no longer the corporate hack. I pulled away and watched Roy in my rear view mirror, trudging back to the office building, a prisoner returning to his cell.

Yep, I quit. Yesterday I went in and I quit. Quit. Quit. Quit. I quit. When a man retires after many decades of service, it's a customary ritual to give him a watch, which is rather odd because for the first time in his life, he doesn't need a watch. Yesterday, in my own little ritual, I came home, took off my watch, and jammed it in the back of a drawer.

I quit. I'm gone, oh, ever so gone from that job, from that sixty hour week, from traveling half the year, from the pointless meetings, the demented leadership, the doomed growth plan. I could have stayed and fought it out, but I'm certain I would have been among the first to be sacrificed to the Negative Cash Flow Gods when the day came for them to demand their due.

I am leaving corporate life for six months, maybe a year. I am going to decompress from twenty years of winding the mainspring a little tighter each day. Each day for twenty years, I have drifted further out of touch with my wife, my family, my neighborhood, my faith and most of all, my self.

Now, I am going to take the time to hug my children, and I am going to take my wife out on dates on Wednesdays, and I am going to join—and use—the gym, and I am going to breathe. And, some day, after I do all of that, I am going to think about what I am going to do next. But right now I am taking a vacation from thinking.

I am concerned that after the six months or year have gone by, after I have smelled the fresh air of freedom, I might never again be of any use to any employer, and that is frankly very scary to me, but I promise myself that, at least for today, I will not be afraid of that. Corporations are an easy way to lose one's self. Many people are willing, even eager to meld into the corporation, to be digested by it, to become the job. But for me, twenty years in corporate life has not given me my identity, it has taken it away. It hasn't enlivened me, it has been a slow death.

Today I will appreciate all the blessings God has given me. I also promise myself not to try to figure out how I will wring even more blessings out of Him in some future day. If I don't climb completely off the hamster wheel, I will have wasted this precious gift of time. Instead, I want to always look back on this time as a turning point, a lightening of the load.

How readily a person can yoke themselves under new burdens the moment they discard the old. It is as if we become accustomed to carrying a certain load, and when we are fortunate enough to get a rest from that load, we lose our balance. I will not do that. I will stay unburdened, at least for now, because I *can*.

I wonder if it would really be so terrible if I could never again become what I once was, if I couldn't return to the atmosphere of corporate life. Wouldn't that be a *good* sign, wouldn't that be a sign that I had adapted to a new atmosphere, had learned to breathe the air in the world outside the corporate biosphere? Let's face it, I wasn't breathing very well inside it anyway.

I want to find that world, and like a space explorer on a new planet, I want to take off my helmet and see if I can survive in the corporate-free atmosphere. Perhaps that world will turn out to be my native planet. I want to see how life is lived outside the confines of the corporation.

I'm free. For the first time in my adult life, I do not have to think, at all, about making a living today, or tomorrow. Someday, yes. But right now in this moment, I can turn off the message that has been repeating itself from my first minute of my first day on my first job, twenty years ago. The message, like the sweet, slightly sinister robotic voice that drones over the speakers at the airport unloading zone, has run through my head, non-stop, for twenty years: "The white (male) zone is for the immediate making of living only. No enjoying, or waiting." I have spent two decades transfixed by and enslaved to that message, trying to obey. The message never pauses long enough for me to get a breath. The message has never stopped. Never, ever.

Now, I have turned that message off. I have quit, quit, quit, and I am going to journey into everyday life. I am going to defy the message: I am not going to make an immediate living. I am going to enjoy, and I am going to wait, to take my time, to appreciate all the good people and things in this wonderful life that God has given me.

It's Tuesday and I don't have to go to work today. I stand up and stretch. I breathe. So, this is what it's like. This is not going to work.

*****

I traveled to quite a few towns during my corporate real estate career, and got to know those towns and meet the townspeople. I've lived in Leucadia since graduating from college, and I have to say, I like Leucadia best.

Leucadia is unpretentious, and I like that. Pretentious places are that way for good reason: they really are nicer. Unpretentious towns, such as Stockton or Mojave or King City are unpretentious because frankly they aren't very nice. Usually this is either because, a) the city founders picked a God-forsaken spot to start a town, like Mojave, or b) they picked a nice enough spot for a town, but planned it all wrong. Leucadia falls in that second category.

Leucadia is the last low-density coastal village in Southern California that is anything close to affordable. We owe much of this to poor planning.

Coastal bluffs rise up at the ocean, then taper downhill to the coast highway, blocking the view of the sea from the road. Yep. Leucadia is right on the ocean, but you can't *see* the ocean. And, the railroad tracks run parallel to the eastern, or inland, side of the highway, obliterating any possibility of development along one whole side of our main road.

There is also a sump, or low spot, which runs parallel to the western, or seaward, side of the highway.

As a result, the driveways, foundations, and parking lots of our downtown businesses flood when it rains.

Corporate Real Estate executives like to locate businesses on busy corners with traffic signals. In Leucadia, there is only one traffic signal because there is only one railroad crossing. Of the four corners at our only intersection in Leucadia, two have railroad tracks running down the middle of them, one is an office building that floods, and the fourth is the city park, which also floods. The park is microscopic and sports exactly two (2) trees. In all fairness, they are both nice trees. Probably because of the flooding. It allows the roots continuous access to groundwater.

A drainage system would obviously help but because the bluff rises up from the beach, then descends to the highway, it blocks not only the view, but any downhill flow of water to the ocean. In the past, it has always been too costly to trench through the bluff and now that it can be afforded, it isn't environmentally feasible.

As a result of our funky commercial district, no chain store businesses—not even Starbucks—have a store in Leucadia. It's all Mom and Pop, or should I say, Moss and Mop. Wet winters make islands of our businesses, when Downtown Leucadia looks like Stiltsville, Florida.

I like all of this about Leucadia. I recommend those towns in a great location with poor planning. They are justifiably unpretentious, which is far more comfortable to me than justifiably pretentious. One can feel the potential in the air, which in Leucadia's case will only be realized when water stops running down hill.

In 1929, after the mistakes of highway and railroad placement were finalized, the Department of Agriculture conducted a study that proved what the local farmers already knew: Leucadia has fabulous soil, Elkhorn Loamy Sand.

Elkhorn Loamy Sand was described by the Department of Agriculture's 1929 Soil Survey, which was undertaken by the Bureau of Chemistry and Soils, in cooperation with the University of California Agricultural Experiment Station. The authors of the Soil Survey were Mr. R. Earl Storie of the University of California and E. J. Alexander of the United States Department of Agriculture:

"Elkhorn Loamy Sand is the important avocado, flower, and vegetable soil of the sandy coastal-plain district which extends from Oceanside south through Carlsbad, Encinitas, and Solana Beach. Elkhorn Loamy Sand has a brown or light reddish-brown loamy sand surface soil, the texture of which is such that it can be tilled at any moisture content. When moist it is very friable... One area of Elkhorn Loamy Sand along the coast at Leucadia has a surface soil without compaction extending to a depth of 4 or 5 feet. Smaller areas of the soil, which have been subject to recent sand movement, are also deep.

"A more or less continuous strip of Elkhorn Loamy Sand extends along the sea front from Oceanside south to Del Mar. This strip is from one-half to 1 ½ miles wide and slopes gently from the sea cliffs to an elevation of approximately 200 feet above sea level."

Because the sump along the highway has collected vegetative debris all those years, the humus on top of the Elkhorn Loamy Sand is several feet thick. Below the humus and Elkhorn Loamy Sand is ground water, and as a result, the eucalyptus trees planted long ago by the side of the highway are some of the largest to be found anywhere.

I've made the same mistakes as the city "planners." Those things which are richest about my life have also been paved over, misplaced, made stagnant and filled with the detritus of untold years. Underneath it all I sense that there is still good soil, awaiting the spark of life. Perhaps I'll find it while I am away from corporate life.

There is another sump in Leucadia, which runs along the top of the coastal hill just inland from the highway. That's where I live. The topsoil on my property is dark black, crumbly, and at least four feet thick. Plants grow so well that in the spring we fill four to six trash cans a week with yard waste.

My property has a storm drain at the low corner and I feel like leaving corporate life has cut a storm drain into the corner of me. The tension of all those years is inexorably draining out of my body this morning. I sense that these fourteen good hours of sleep are a mere down payment on the process of peeling back the layers of stress, overwork and the shell I have built up. Now it can all fall off. I surrender. Eventually good things will take root and grow in me, and in my family.

Today, for once in a thousand Tuesdays, I get to finish sleeping, wake up, feel wonderful, ask myself what I want to do today, and then just go and do it, without worrying about how my actions will be misinterpreted by my boss, or the Human Resources Department.

*****

What I am going to do is to take a little journey to a place which itself took a little journey after serving as host to hobo, wayfarer and wanderer for many decades. A place called the Pannikin.

As one would expect, Leucadia wasn't planned with a community center of any kind. Our sense of community, if any, is defined by our lack of community sense. A few years back, a local businessman bought an old railroad depot, circa 1895, had it moved to Leucadia, and opened a coffee shop in it, "The Pannikin." Now, if Leucadia has a "community center," The Pannikin is it.

I take my coffee upstairs to the former train platform. There are enormous wooden sliding doors through which passed the freight and passengers of another time. The doors are partly covered with handbills announcing yoga and massage and seeking roommates and house-sitting opportunities.

The vintage graffiti in the building evokes the stories of people long gone. I imagine travelers having to layover after all the day's trains have departed, arranging with an agreeable stationmaster to spend the night inside the depot, characters from a Steinbeck tale. Or perhaps the stationmaster is not so agreeable, or the travelers so presentable, and after the doors are closed and locked, hobos emerge from hiding places among the shipping crates. In any case, their stories are written and still survive inside this building, if anyone cares to look up from their Mocha Frappe Latte with Double Whip, on The Side.

Long ago, early last century, a lump of coal from stove or coal car became a writing implement. Idle, lonely, bored, someone stacked empty crates and climbed up into the rafters to neatly scribe: H.I.A. 1903. The letters are visible above me as I sip my coffee.

Seven years later, using a pocketknife, B.L.W. carved initials into the adjacent rafter: B.L.W. 8/17/10. Adjacent to that, C.L.W. scribed his initials in coal. One used coal and one used a pocketknife. Were they brothers?

Two years later, Norman Abell, far from home, took a lump of coal, licked it, and wrote on the door in elaborate script,

Norman Abell
Tombstone Ariz.
Sept. 12, 1912
Tourist

Was the stationmaster looking the other way, when he did that, or long gone home to bed and hearth? Does the home yet stand somewhere here in our little village of Leucadia by the sea?

Cryptic insignias resembling cattle brands yet remain: A backward "J" linked to a "V", an "E" with an extended center tine, the letters "GZ" inside a circle, a "J" linked to an "R" with a shallow "V." The calling cards of forgotten men, long dead.

On one of the freight doors is written,

L. L. B. Edward
San Bernardino

On another door, inside a valentine,

V. R.

\+

John Steeg
June 3rd, 1927

Did they marry?   Were there children, now senior citizens?

Also this:

J. E. Walsh. Gallup NM 1906

And from a nearby town:

VISTA, CAL
RAY

I look at the names and initials, each written during an idle moment in a forgotten life, each life now certainly past. How did those lives go? What became of them on their travels? What was their end and resting place, do they yet continue through their descendants in some fashion? How did those children "turn out"? Are their descendants among us today? Is the Abell clan still in Tombstone, are there any Walsh's left in Gallup?

Over the years, my work has taken me to Tombstone and Gallup and San Bernardino and Vista and all points between and beyond and now, I am home in Leucadia. Home to stay and, I hope and pray, to live a life that is unpretentious, and significant, and real. The Leucadia Life. I am home at last.

Impulsively I look up the last name "Edward" in San Bernardino and "Abell" in Tombstone. There are no "Abells" in Tombstone, but there is one "Edward" in the San Bernardino area. The harried mother who answers tells me they moved to San Bernardino ten years ago, have no relatives nearby, and as far as she knows, no ancestor with the initials "L. L. B."

FEBRUARY

February is an in-between month, when the holidays are past and put away, and the spring weather hasn't yet arrived. For me, this February is an opportunity to appreciate and assess what I have, what works, and to consider what I might change, come spring.

Every day of my life for as long as I can remember, I have thought about what I will do in the world to make a living. Every day of my working life I have tried to do what it takes to make that living, and to do it better and better. Every single day.

And now, there is a chapter in my life where I am going to take a break from that and *not think* about how in the world I will make a living. I will think about it again some day, I know. But now, for once, I am taking a break. I almost feel—no, I *do* feel—that I need the break from worrying about how to make a living more than I need the break from making a living.

I am going to not think. For now, I get to taste what it is like for those old guys in coveralls who spend the day puttering around the house and driving their wives crazy while not thinking about making a living any more. I get to do that in a forty-one-year-old body instead of a seventy-one-year-old body, and I am so blessed by that.

I compose a list of ideas, of guiding words for these months to come, and make a small poster, which I frame and hang. It's a poem of sorts, which becomes simpler and simpler, as each line has only one word, and each word has one fewer letter than the word above it, nine words and a singular punctuation:

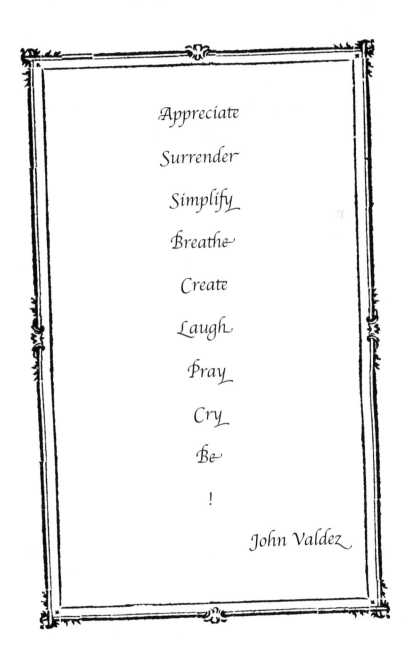

Appreciate

Surrender

Simplify

Breathe

Create

Laugh

Pray

Cry

Be

!

John Valdez

JOHN VALDEZ

We live in a thirty-five-year-old house on a quarter acre of flat property, not far from the beach. There are a dozen or two houses in this little neighborhood. We bought our house ten years ago and it's a good house, but I have ten years of neglected "honey-dos" to catch up on. I hope to get close to the end of that list.

Whereas the average home in this part of California changes hands about every five years, the average home on our street sells about every twenty-two years. In fact, half a dozen of the houses are still occupied by the original owners. Every few years, somebody on the street will list their house for sale, and then go out to look for another place to live. The house will sell within a few days, or even a few hours. The seller keeps looking for the other place to live. When they see larger houses stuck right next together on tiny graded orange clay lots, with a few strategically planted trees struggling to survive, they remember the large-lobed, seventy-year-old avocados of home—still bearing fruit—they cancel the sale, and the listing, and they stay.

We remodeled the inside of our home before we moved in, but now as I look at the outside of the house, I am reminded that we never really did any outside landscaping improvements.

It's the trees and the plants and the land that keep us here, not the house. The house, while nice, is frankly undersized for our family of six. There were four of us when we bought the house, but two more have since arrived.

For ten years, my wife, Katie, has been faithfully watering the plants with a hose, her thumb over the end to control the flow. On watering day, she has been moving sprinklers around on the lawn every few minutes, all day long.

As I look around the perimeter of the house I notice some little piles of orange pellets on the ground. Termites. I take a stick and jab it into an eave. The stick punctures through the membrane of paint, spilling a cache of pellets onto the ground at my feet.

The paint is weathered and worn everywhere under the eaves, and the stucco is peeling off the side of the house in several places.

When we bought the house, the prior owner warned us about Mister Boyer, the neighbor behind us. Mr. Boyer was in his eighties and quite friendly. The fence we shared with Mr. Boyer had become a heap of ivy growing over collapsed sections of lattice, with a few surviving metal fence posts poking defiantly into the air. The ivy had grown out of control, unkempt for decades. Mr. Boyer liked it that way: He hid in the biomass of the "fence" to spy on Katie, who is beautiful. Boyer the Voyeur. A few months after we moved in, Mr. Boyer's wife passed away, and a few weeks after that, he moved in with a lady friend out in Rancho Santa Fe.

The heap of a fence had remained after Mr. Voyeur moved, and had grown to a critical mass, to the point that now the shear weight of the thing was causing it to collapse under itself, and we had to prop it up with two-by-fours to keep it from falling into our yard. It was a losing battle and if we didn't act, would be a matter of time until we would wake up to find our back yard buried under the collapse. The fence and its heap of ivy is a hundred and fifteen feet long, six feet high and about six feet wide. Not the sort of problem to be tackled with a pair of garden shears and a stack of trash cans.

The space between the house and the garage is roofed in and open ended, creating a breezeway. When we bought the house, we installed a skylight in the breezeway roof to bring in light.

However, there is some drywall up inside the tunnel of the skylight that I never got around to priming or painting. When I look up, which I try not to do any more because it drives me crazy, I see a splatter of joint compound on the raw drywall that resembles a butterfly. I have been looking at that thing for ten years and for ten years I have been saying, "This weekend, I will get up in that skylight and paint over it." I am ten years older now and the butterfly is ten years older and I've planned and failed to paint it out five hundred and twenty times.

It's time to buy some coveralls. No more planning and then not doing. In fact, I'm just going to *do* all day long and not *plan* any more. When I reach the end of my backlogged list of plans, I'm confident I can easily come up with more, but for now I'm done being paralyzed by way too many *plans* and way too little *do*.

Coastal Southern California is noted for especially bad soil. It is hard, orange acidic clay permeated with grapefruit-sized boulders.

But my house in Leucadia is different. The best thing about my house is the soil. Before the land was converted to housing, there had been an avocado grove here for thirty-five years. There are thirty-five years of avocado leaves composted into that Elkhorn Loamy Sand. It gets better still: Prior to the installation of the storm drain that was installed when the houses were built, all the detritus from the surrounding lands settled and composted here, starting from around the time life began on earth. Plants grow incredibly well here in the four-foot thick topsoil. It's like "Land of the Giants." When we buy a plant at the nursery and stick it in the ground, the new leaves grow to four times the size of the old leaves, and two shades deeper green. Within a year, we have to hack away at it to keep it under control.

The homes in the neighborhood are all on septic systems rather than connected to the sewer. From time to time someone's system will overload, and Clyde is summoned. He arrives with his monstrous tanker truck with the elephant painted on the side. The elephant is depicted slurping, well … poop, out of a hole in the ground with his trunk. The license plate on the truck reads, "P U GONE."

Clyde has a nice little monopoly going. When the contents of the toilet bowl swirl about with no real commitment to actually flushing down, we call Clyde, who stands out in our yard pumping the septic tank and extorting us while complaining about how expensive everything in the world is.

Clyde has traded away the possibility of ever having a wife for pure cash wealth. Accordingly, he has allowed himself to go fully to seed. I was behind him in line at the bank one day when he deposited a wad of cash, his pants sagging well below his fanny crack, revealing the rimply vertical channel that is a symbol both of the source of his wealth and the reason for his solitude.

With the six of us living in this tiny house, Clyde makes the rounds here frequently . Had I had more daughters and fewer sons, I'm sure we would see even more of Clyde, making him even wealthier.

Michael, our oldest son, has just turned fourteen. The great hormonal onslaught is rumbling through his every cell. It has affected his speech, causing him to oftentimes mumble in a monotone like Marlon Brando and construct his sentences into one polysyllabic word: *Mom-can-I-go-over-to-Jasons-just-hang-out-whatever?*

He remains however, a sweet, kind thoughtful and sensitive person, except for one rather quirky and relentless behavior: He squeezes children's heads.

One could define our entire family dynamic over the years from the vantage of this behavior. It started when Michael met his little brother, our second child Alex, at the hospital. When Mikey met Alex, he smiled, reached over, and squeezed Alex's head, palming the spongy-skulled little newborn like a cantaloupe. This continues today. If Mikey is intrigued by the size and shape of someone's head, he will reach over and start squeezing it. The size, shape and what he calls the "Booska Index" are the determining considerations of which heads he squeezes.

Michael will squeeze the head of any child with a "Booska Eight" or better, whether that child is known to him or not. This mysterious "Booska" quality seems to be influenced not only by the size and shape of the head, but by how "fuzzy" the head is, that is, how much the hair

41

sticks out and how fine each of the individual hair strands are. The angle at which the head is upheld by its owner also seems to be a factor.

I can't explain it. Perhaps it is some remnant of instinct leftover from previous generations, designed, I might guess, to somehow express sibling dominance.

I've talked to him about it. I've warned him about it. I've begged him about it, I've threatened him about it, but in the end, he is unable to stop himself, or be stopped, regardless of the consequences. Katie and I have had to conclude that we are the parents of a person who is kind, intelligent, thoughtful, capable, and who also squeezes people's heads.

Unfortunately for Alex, he was born at a Booska Nine level and as his fuzzy little yellow hair grew in, he developed into a full-blown Booska Ten. By the time Alex was four, his hair stuck straight out in all directions, very much like the celebrated Dr. Einstein. (Michael says Einstein was an honorary Booska Ten, but only *honorary* because adults can't actually have a Booska Index.)

Furthermore, because of the constant squeezing attacks, the defensive angle at which poor Alex holds his head has become quite ducky-like: squat, low, defensive, ready to snap, like an Easter Ducky Chick.

Alex is eleven and a half now, and I hope that as he reaches teenhood, the relationship between him and

Michael will shift from being based upon Michael squeezing Alex's head to something, anything, more significant.

Alex is a kind, intelligent, still-fuzzyheaded boy with large beautiful brown eyes and a sweet scratchy voice, made so by endless alarm calls — quacks if you will — from Michael's relentless head squeezing attacks. Alex is much smaller than Michael and has developed excellent verbal skills to compensate. He inflicts verbal attacks with surgical strike precision. These bomblets are large enough to damage the opponent yet small enough not to be detected by the parental radar, resulting in parental rebuke. He is a genius. Sometimes his bombing strikes continue round the clock for days on end.

Whereas Michael squeezes heads, Alex spends his time launching things and watching how they land. When the landing of the things is particularly interesting, he reports on it to whoever will listen. That's what Alex does with his life.

Shawn, our third son and child, was born when Alex was two and a half and Mikey was five. We were so excited when we were expecting our third child, but no one was more excited than Alex. He was very sweet to Katie and seemed to post himself at her side around the clock to await the arrival of the new little baby. Thinking back, I now have the notion that Alex's motivation in all of this was the desperate hope that the new baby would have a higher Booska Index, thereby taking some of the head squeezing pressure off of himself. Unfortunately for Alex, Shawn scores a disappointing Booska Four-Point-Five.

Shawn is now almost nine, but from his first moments in life, I could tell that he could tell that, like his father, he was the youngest of three brothers and he better start peddling fast and hard, now, if he was to have any chance of ever keeping up.

Shawn has become a big strong brute of a guy, and like Michael, is impervious to physical pain. Yet he is a gentle sweet soul, kind to others, insightful, sensitive, and caring. Inasmuch as he has a low Booska Index, Michael leaves Shawn's head alone for the most part and Alex, lacking a brother to take some of the brunt of Mikey's headsqueezings, uses Shawn for recreational verbal abuse target practice:

"Shawn, you are so *stupid*."

"Why?"

"Uhh! I can't even explain. You'd never understand..."

Once in a great while, when Alex proffers one of his little bomblets on Shawn, Shawn will ignite. Shawn is a rather husky fellow and it isn't beyond him to throw Alex across the room, then advance on the crumpled smudgemark of Alex, declaring his intent to kill him. Alex, innocent, palms up, mystified that such a teeny bomblet could ignite such a response, wisely seeks a diplomatic resolution to the conflict through Katie and I, while typically including demands for the specific punishment we ought to mete out to Shawn. In this fashion, one might say that there is a certain equilibrium of power.

Due to Shawn's low Booska Index, Alex continued to take the full brunt of Mikey's relentless head squeezing for seven long years.

Then Vanessa, our fourth child and only girl was born. We waved Mikey off for as long as we could — about and hour and a half — then Mikey breached our defenses, rushed in, squeezed Vanessa's head and retreated, like a jackal that had nipped at prey. The load came off of Alex that day.

Remarkably, Vanessa is another Booska Ten. With Vanessa, I have begun to see what Michael means about being "squeezable." She has an enormous fuzzy fluffy white head of hair that people just cannot resist squeezing.

People tell me that Vanessa is one of the prettiest creatures on earth. Frankly, they're right.

I am not entirely comfortable with the fact that Vanessa is one of the prettiest creatures on earth. I do take comfort in the fact that she is smart, wily, and easily provoked into relentlessly, smilingly, beating her big brothers into a giggling pulp. I also take comfort in knowing that her big brothers have made it widely known that they will gleefully pound the snot out of anyone who would cause her any harm.

Michael, fourteen. Alex, eleven and a half. Shawn, nearly nine. Vanessa, almost five. Wonderful kids. They are changing and growing so fast, and I am grateful that I don't have to miss out on this one little section of their lives. I'm home. I get to be with them, watch them, enjoy them. I get to act and feel like a grandfather, but with my own *kids*. I don't have to wait. I have time. I can breathe. I can be patient. I can appreciate who they are. I can lead them and teach them and mold them.

✳✳✳✳✳

It's dinnertime.

"Can somebody bring the forks?" I say. "I want a fork, who has a fork? Bring a whole bunch of them. Do we have enough clean forks? Okay, c'mon guys, let's pray. Make a circle. Did everybody wash their hands? Stop whatever you're doing and come in here so we can pray. Get in here. Everybody's waiting."

We stand in a circle and hold hands, well not really: Michael palms Vanessa's head like a basketball, Vanessa leans against my wife, Alex holds Shawn's wrist, not his hand.

"Alex," I say, "hold Shawn's hand."

Alex shoots a desperate look at me, signaling that he's going to be sick to his stomach.

"His hand is all *gross*," he says. "He's been *wiping* things on it." He starts to go into detail but I cut him off.

"Shawn, didn't you wash your hands?" I ask.

"You told me to stop whatever I was doing and come in here so we can pray."

"Okay, well, we'll pray. Let's say grace. Everybody settle down and be quiet. Michael, would you like to pray, please?"

He's fourteen.

He's hungry.

He's trapped.

In that monotone 'tweenage drone, he prays as though placing an order at God's Fast-Food Drive-Through window: *"God, okay, uhm, thanks-for-everything-and-everything-and-uh, I-pray-you-will-make-everything-be-uhm, good, or whatever. Whatever-you-wanna-do. And that I'll-do-really-good-on-my-science-test-tomorrow. Thanks for this food. Amen."*

"Don't forget to pray for Mrs. Z and Mrs. Randall," Katie reminds him.

He files an addendum. *"...and uh, we-pray-for-Mrs. Z and-Mrs. Randall."*

The instant we say, "Amen," their hands recoil and they rub them as though they'd just been let out of handcuffs.

We sit down and plates clank, chairs scrape, (The boys don't actually sit on the chairs. Rather, they sit on the edge of the chairs, with their legs pointing away from the table, I suppose it's in order to facilitate a quick *"Thank-you-mom-can-I-be-excused"* getaway.) Sauerkraut is draped, slurped, and dangled obliviously around mouths; body gases release sporadically at high pressure, unfettered and unacknowledged. Frantic to feed himself, one kid accidentally hits another in the temple with his elbow. I grit my teeth and dig my nails into the edge of the table. My water glass is missing Somewhere Out There on the table, swirling with someone else's backwash. I focus my attention on the solid food on the plate in front of me.

I try to spear a piece of Polska, but just as I do, someone shoves the table aside about a quarter of an inch. My fork hits the sausage a degree or two away from top dead center so it shoots out and splats into my chest, then drops onto my lap. No one notices.

Shawn falls abruptly off his chair, a not-uncommon consequence of that curious, sideways, off-center sitting style. The chair tips over, onto him. He remains on the floor for a while, flat on his hiney, giggling.

When he ascends back to the table, I call a Time Out. There is a moment of silence. "Children, you are eating like pigs. Would you consider slowing down, just a bit?

Please?" Another moment of silence, then the chaos resumes, unabated.

As I watch the next dozen or so bites, I witness twelve distinct, treacherous, creative, never-before-seen methods for getting food into the mouth. Now, Katie and I have been at this parenting job for fourteen years, about eighty man-years between us when we count up the ages of our children, yet I do not see encouraging progress. Katie implores me to look past it, engage them in discussions about the events of the day, and they'll eventually turn out okay.

She asks Michael to please go turn off his bedroom light. He blames the light on Alex. Alex shoots the blame back at Michael. They go back and forth like this for a while, and no one budges from the table. Their voices raise, their veins bulge. Finally, my weary wife decides it's not worth it and gets up and goes to turn off the bedroom light herself. They don't notice that she is gone and the bickering continues unimpeded. The question of Who Left The Light On has become a matter of principle, of character, of Who Remembers Correctly, and of Who Is Retarded.

I had clipped an article about some new research and discoveries about Ludwig Von Beethoven, and had planned an intellectual and high-minded conversation among enlightened individuals, respectfully agreeing to disagree about some of the fine points of things Beethoven.

Taking my wife's suggestion, I decide to try it. I produce the Beethoven clipping from the paper. "Hey, kids," I begin, and one of them—okay it was Shawn—turns his head toward me, looks me straight in the eye, smiles widely, then belches loudly. Hysterics break out all around the table, but not from me. My wife hides a giggle in her palm. That's it.

I stand up and walk out of the house, leaving my plate behind and, somewhere, my water glass. Silence descends behind me.

We have an old travel trailer that we occasionally go camping in, and I unlock it and turn on some lights.

I'm still hungry, but I am *not* going back in there to retrieve my abandoned dinner. I look through the cupboards. I find a can of tuna. I find the "old reliable" can opener—the ugly one that works better than the fancy one in the house.

Then, I open a drawer and there, staring up at me, is my backpacking fork.

I made my backpacking fork when I was nineteen. I pull it out of the drawer and hold it in my hand. It had been a perfectly fine fork before I got hold of it, with long tines and a normal handle. I remember how Katie—who was then my girlfriend—watched, puzzled, as I hacksawed off the handle and smoothed down the burrs on a buffer-grinder. One millimeter shorter and it would be too short to use. One millimeter longer and it would be more to carry than absolutely necessary. Now, more than two decades later, it still feels familiar to my hand.

I open the tuna and dig into it with the fork. I flash back, nineteen years old again:

I am inside my small tent in the Borrego Desert. Box Canyon. March, many years ago. My friend Phillip Shaw and I have hiked about sixty miles over the last few days with many, many miles to go. I put the tent up just before the sun dropped, and when it did drop, the temperature dove and the wind came up. Now, with an unexpected contentment, I am opening up a can of tuna for dinner, working the simple can opener from my Swiss Army Knife around the perimeter of the lid, little by little, an eighth-of-an-inch at a time. The wind beats the small tent down on top of my head and shoulders. It pops back up. Eventually, I pry off the lid and sink my fork—this same fork—down into the oily, brownish scraps of tuna. Famished, I take an enormous bite. It's delicious. I had been looking forward to this moment for the last five miles, and all during the time I was setting up camp.

I hear a gale of wind ripping down the canyon toward me. I brace. The wind slams against the tiny tent and flattens it down against my head. I lean forward to wait it out. Outside, a million stars pierce a pitch-black sky, unseen. Inside my tent, I am safe. I am warm. I am comfortable. Let the wind blow. I have my dinner.

I finish the tuna, wipe the fork clean with my mouth — backpacker style — and walk back into the house. Katie is playing the piano. Alex is practicing his clarinet. Shawn, wearing headphones, practices electronic drums. Though the pulse of this place is sometimes out of control, the sound of Shawn's steady tap-tap-tapping is now delightfully reassuring. The non-issues are just that. We'll have a little talk sometime soon. Vanessa is playing "dress ups." Mikey, taking a break from homework, practices guitar. I have much to be grateful for, including a large and wonderful family. I'm not nineteen years old anymore.

Stacks of dirty dishes cover the kitchen counter. Oh well. First, I wash and dry my fork and place it in my shirt pocket, then I start in on the other dishes. Life in the desert inside a turbulent tent isn't much of a life. That life is gone, as it should be. But it's nice to know that I still have my backpacking fork.

It sometimes surprises me to realize that the beautiful, wonderful woman I am married to, is my high school girlfriend; the girl I married when she was nineteen. She is as beautiful as ever, and that is not a sweet sentimentality, but a fortunate fact. She is the beneficiary of good genes, a blonde Czech. These women are strong, healthy, vigorous, gorgeous, and they *stay* that way. They are not only physically tough, but mentally tough as well. Once Katherine is determined about something, the only question for me is to decide whether I prefer to applaud her as she charges past, or stand in the way to discuss it and get flattened.

I have learned to choose to applaud her. To be flattened is one thing, but to be flattened by a tiny, sweet, dainty beautiful girl with large and lovely emerald eyes and a soft lovely voice is much, much more embarrassing.

Katie is turning forty this month. We met when she was sixteen, and I have never known a kinder person. She is disarmingly pretty and absolutely without pretense. She has a sweet, enchanting voice, and when she talks to animals, they visibly soften, begin to relax, and listen. They lower their animal defenses and relate to her not as an animal to a human, but simply, and openly, as one living being to another living being. The barriers vanish and they are, for that moment, not an animal but simply a better living being.

I have always found Katie to be irresistible. I can't stay away from her. She has a beautiful, fine-featured face with those big emerald-green eyes, a sunrise smile with sweet delicate lips and a full head of beautiful blonde hair.

She is also the toughest and strongest minded person I have ever met. She has very particular ideas about things, especially when it comes to how things should *look*. When she digs in her heels, there is no unlocking her. Once she decides to dig in and fight, she will stubbornly resist any outcome but her own, regardless of the consequences to herself or others. When we quarrel, it is impossible for me to stay mad at her because she is absolutely irresistible. I try my very best to give her what ever she wants.

What she wants for her fortieth birthday is to have the extended family over for cake, ice cream and presents. The presents she wants are gift certificates to a particular gallery, where she wishes to select some framed art prints for the walls of our home.

She says, "I want you to use those little placemats that have the gardening pots and the tulips on them, not the daisies - I know you - I want the pots and the tulips. If you could get the good glasses down from the cupboard but don't let the kids have them and especially Bobby because last time he was here he got in the kids' room and tore it up and I don't think he's quite ready for a big boy glass but we still have a plastic dribble cup in the back of that drawer." She points to the drawer.

I smile. "Honey, the party is going to be fine. Don't worry about it."

"I'm not worried, I just want certain things for my fortieth birthday party, and I think I should be able to ask for them."

"But if I am going to do this party for you, shouldn't I be able to have things a certain way, too? I mean, I'm the one who has to do everything."

"I'm not asking you to do that much."

"Well, let me just GIVE you this party, from me, in my way. Let it be something that comes from me that I do for you, okay?"

The day of the party comes. Guests are due at 6:30. It is six o'clock. Katie comes home to find me standing on a kitchen chair, scotch-taping one end of a roll of crepe-paper streamers to the hanging lamp over the dining table. I turn, smile, and wave. I know there are dirty dishes spread out on the counter and down into the sink, but the dishwasher is empty and most of them will probably fit in it.

She inhales, tensing up. She does not exhale. Tightly she says, "What are you doing?"

"I'm decorating for your party."

More inhalation. "I'm not a big fan of crepe-paper streamers," she confides quietly to the floor.

"But it's a *party!*"

"...not very classy..." (Inhales again. Does this woman ever *breathe?*) "People are going to be here soon," she mutters.

"I know, that's why I'm *decorating.*"

"The kitchen is a mess," she says. She pauses. Her shoulders slump forward, her head drops, and she slogs into the kitchen, a martyr, cleaning up for her own fortieth birthday party.

"Don't do that, honey," I say.

"Well, who else is going to do it?"

"Kids," I yell, "can you come on out here? We need some help." Then to Katie, "Please, Katie, leave that."

"I don't want the kids cleaning up. They'll just make a bigger mess."

"*I'll* clean it up. Kids, would you guys like to put up these streamers so I can clean the kitchen?"

"Sure, Dad." The kids can tell that the boat is sinking.

"Go on, honey, get ready. People will be here soon." I attempt to escort her to the hall.

"I know, that's why I'm cleaning up." She snaps a pillow up off the floor and fluffs it, then walks into the living room and jams it onto the couch. "I can't do this..." She starts to hyperventilate. "I can't do this..."

I laugh and hug her and try to kiss her but she pulls away, panicked. "I can't breathe with you kissing me like that." Then, realizing something else is amiss, she winces and asks, "What about the food?"

"I already bought a cake and I was gonna go get some ice cream after I ordered pizza. What kind of pizza would you like?"

"Dad, Shawn is wrecking the streamers," Alex reports.

"Not just now, Alex. We can talk about that while mom is in the bedroom getting ready."

"I can't stay here. I have to go," she says.

"Okay, Honey. You go get ready."

"I'm leaving. I can't stand this."

"Honey..."

"It's just that I don't want my birthday to be like this."

"Everything will be fine, trust me. This is our family. They understand. I love you. I want you to have a happy birthday. I even have the *tulip* placemats out. Not the daisies."

But the "tulip placemat" line isn't quite enough to do it. She turns and dashes into the bedroom. A few minutes later, red eyed, she emerges, pulling on her coat. "I'm going to a movie," she murmurs, and with finality, closes the door behind her.

"Well," I say, turning to the kids and giggling stupidly, "what kind of pizza do you kids want?"

I throw the dishes into the washer and ask Michael to order the pizza while I run to the store for ice cream, but since Katie is gone, I'm really not quite sure why I am getting ice cream.

When I return from the store, I hide the last bit of mess. Fine. Looks like a party to me. Oh, music. I'll put some music on. I have *The 25 Greatest Polka Hits of All Time, Vol. II* that I like to put on for parties. This party isn't quite ready for that yet, so I put on jazz instead.

The doorbell rings. It's "Donpa," Katie's father, and his wife, "Grandma Jan." We hug and airkiss and say hello and I invite them in. Jan asks what's wrong. Donpa looks concerned. "Nothing," I say. "Nice ... uh ... 'outfit' Donpa."

"Old fashions please me best."

Indeed they do. "Right. Come on in," I say.

Donpa catches the sound of the jazz piano, and observes, "He makes sweet music with th' enameled stones."

"Thank you. It's Oscar Peterson."

Jan says, "I saw Oscar Peterson in a live concert in Chicago ... golly, that was a long time ago ... "

A few years after Katie's mother died, we introduced Donpa to Jan. Little did Jan know that Don had a closetful of outfits like the one he arrived in for their first date, which was a Shakespeare play. Despite that odd start, Don and Jan have been inseparable from the moment they met.

To be clear, Don is a completely rational and high-functioning human being, a genius's genius, a world-renowned theoretical physicist and student of language, who delights in all things Shakespearean and happens to get a huge kick out of quoting The Bard, in context.

They've just come from another Shakespeare Festival and he's wearing an audacious velour cap, complete with feather, a long-sleeved puffy shirt with deep v-neck, mercifully not-too-tight tights, and those pointy little shoes; she's in a tailored suit with matching handbag and shoes, her hair, makeup and nails immaculate, and his cape gallantly but dishevonedly draped over her shoulders.

I take their cape and coat and purse and cap and ask him about the Shakespeare Festival, then offer them chips and something to drink. Donpa goes to check the labels on the beer. Jan turns to me and asks, "Where's Katie?"

"She's not here."

"Where is she?"

I start to giggle stupidly. "I don't know."

"When is she coming back?"

"I don't know."

"Why did she leave?"

"She didn't like it here."

"*Where* is Katie?" Donpa asks, back with his beer.

My giggle has moved out of my belly and up my neck and out my mouth and has begun to sort of hang stupidly off the front of my face, swinging around out there, sort of an embarrassing dangler. I ... I wish it weren't dangling there but I don't see any way to cut it off without drawing even more attention to it, so with a stupid face, I say to my wife's father, "I don't know."

"She got mad and left," Jan explains.

"Oh. Hmmm." Donpa's mouth is closed and his hands are on his hips, elbows pointing behind him. "Hmmm." His head bobs up and down, he slowly blinks, then asks, "Why did she get mad?"

"I don't know why."

"Every why hath a wherefore."

"Well, I guess she didn't like my party. She didn't like how I did her party."

"What didn't she like?" He smiles. "An honest tale speeds best plainly told."

So I go into detail about the streamers and the pizza and the tulip placemats and the mess in the kitchen while he patiently sips his pint of beer. As I conclude, he turns to Jan and with a twinkle in his eye and his thumb pointed at me, says to her, like an aside in a play, "He draweth out the thread of his verbosity finer than the staple of his argument." I'm not positive, but I think he's teasing me.

Don examines the glass, the detail of the bubbles, the mound of foam. "O Katie, O tiger's heart wrapped in a woman's hide!"

"That's Katie."

"Was ever woman in this humor wooed? Was ever woman in this humor won? Alas, how love can trifle with itself." He reverently takes the glass to his lips and steadily drinks the rest of the pint down, wipes his mouth with the back of his sleeve, and says something about a felony for small beer. Then he wraps his arm around Jan, smiles broadly at me and says, "We may pity, though not pardon thee, Valdez. But we will speak of it no more. Let the gaudy, babbling, and remorseful day be crept into the bosom of the sea."

So I do. Whatever that means.

The party turns out to be unforgettably fun. We balance nickels on our nose, have a conga line, and do the hokey pokey. Even Jan. Everyone talks understandingly and endearingly of Katie: beautiful, gentle, wonderful, stubborn, irresistible Katie. We miss her, but appreciate her all the more. She gets a lot of gift certificates to that gallery (I assume, based on the unopened birthday cards) and Bobby, as far as I know, doesn't destroy anything.

Hours later and a bit too late, I put on my *25 Greatest Polka Hits of All Time, Vol. II* album. There is not enough energy left in the room to dance, so it sort of ends the

61

party. Oh well. Donpa turns to Jan and says, "Arise, my dearest, we depart, for you and I are past our dancing days."

Don posts himself at the door, bowing and flourishing his hat to each departing guest. When the last of them have gone, I thank him for smoothing things over and he says, "Harp not on that string, dear fellow. You are no worse a husband than the best of men." He pats my shoulder and smiles beery breath onto me.

The front gate swings open, Katie walks in.

"Happy 40th, Honey," Jan says, "I would have left, too."

I walk toward her, we hug.

Donpa turns to Jan and gently says, "Love comforteth like sunshine after rain." Then he announces, "We depart! Unbidden guests are often welcomest when they are gone."

Jan says, "Don't you want to give Katie her present?"

He smiles, produces an envelope, bows, and hands it to Katie.

Katie knows it's forty one-dollar bills. "Thank you, Dad."

"Remuneration! O! That's the Latin word for three farthings. Now put thy money in thy purse."

We say goodbye and watch them totter off into the night as he sings an ancient and very ribald or very noble ditty, depending on how you take it.

"I love you, John." Katie pulls me close.

"I love you, too."

But I am not going to tell her what art prints she should buy with those gift certificates.

*****

Alex entered an electric motor experiment in the school Science Fair this year and was selected as a finalist for an award from the Armed Forces Communications and Electronics Association. You know, the "AFCEA."

This is what his Science Fair Project consists of: The actual Project itself is a six-inch-long block of two-by-four wood, with two short pieces of coat hanger wire sticking into it. The block of wood could easily fit into the average glove compartment. When we show it, we lay out an assortment of batteries, magnets, and wire on the table.

That's it. That's the whole thing.

So to make it interesting, Katie made a Display Board that is an award-worthy work of art in its own right. Essentially, the Award Worthy Display Board touts the wonders of the Block of Wood with Two Wires Sticking Into It.

And then there is the Written Report. The essence of the Written Report is, "I don't understand electric motors because, when I used just one battery, the motor went slow, so I used two batteries and the motor went even slower. When I used three batteries, it went really, really fast. Sometimes. But not always. I don't get it."

The AFCEA (AFF·see·ya) is having their annual symposium now, and invited him to display and discuss his Project between 10:00 a.m. and 4:00 p.m. today. He's been excused from school and has a fresh haircut and is wearing a little man-coat and tie and he looks great.

However, last weekend Shawn fell off his skateboard, and from the way his fingers angled off in a new direction, it was pretty obvious he'd broken a few things in his hand. We rushed down to the Emergency Room and they put it in a splint and took some X-rays and gave us the X-rays and said we should see a Pediatric Orthopedist. They said, "Be sure to bring the X-rays to your appointment with the Pediatric Orthopedist. They'll want to look at these because there's growth plate involvement." That is not a good thing. So they put on a temporary cast and we have a 9:45 a.m. appointment for today at Children's Hospital.

Plus Alex is bringing his parakeet who is sitting on a washcloth in a little brown cardboard box. He bred and hand-raised and hand-fed some parakeets and kept the best one for himself. Little Petey isn't feeling well so we have to go to the vet, not just any vet apparently, but a *bird* vet, which fortunately is not far from the AFCEA.

Well, this will work out pretty well. I'll take Shawn to Children's Hospital for his 9:45 appointment, and then take Alex to the AFCEA symposium that starts at 10:00. They're both in the same part of town. Shawn may be a little late, but that's okay. Oh, and then to the vet afterwards. The bird vet.

We pull into the hospital parking lot at 9:45 and I realize at that moment that I forgot to bring Shawn's X-Rays. Shoot.

By 10:00 we've parked and are in the building. I'm ready to explain about the X-rays to the receptionist but before I can, she explains to me to "please have a seat and wait to be called" and "Is that a pet? You can't bring pets in here."

I watch Alex's back as he retreats through the exit doors, the shoulders of his tiny coat on his tiny body curled forward over his little friend, his great fuzzy blondish blob of hair whisping upward and outward in all directions. The cute and vulnerable back of neck. The doors swipe closed behind him. Then Shawn and the nurse and I go through the paperwork and the explanations and we have to wait for an available X-ray Tech to take Shawn's X-rays all over again thanks to me and time is going by and Alex is sitting on the bench in the sunshine outside the hospital cradling his bird in his hands and missing the AFCEA symposium. And the doctor has to work us in to his schedule because we missed our 9:45 appointment and showed up without X-Rays.

Alex, the scientist, waits stoically outside the hospital in his coat and tie, his parakeet in his hands, and time slips away. I go out to check on him and he's curled over his pet and when I get his attention, he slowly uncurls himself and looks up to me with huge, worried, dreary brown eyes. The parakeet is nestled in Alex's cupped hands, his feathers puffed out, his eyes closed, his tiny body shaking from time to time. Alex has been stroking Petey's back with one finger, and praying. Alex and Petey go everywhere together and Alex has even trained Petey to fly to his finger. Alex is always happy when Petey is with him, but now, Alex is not happy. He asks if he can skip the AFCEA symposium and go straight to the vet. "It won't be long now," I tell him.

It's 10:30, then 11:30. Alex and Petey are marooned outside the hospital, and we would have been finished and on our way to the bird vet a long ago if I had remembered those X-rays.

At noon I go out to check on Alex and Petey. Alex's back is toward me. The little sloped shoulders of his coat are shaking.

"Hey, Alex."

His big brown beautiful eyes are brimmed with tears.

"Oh. I'm so sorry."

He needs to tell what happened, with his scratchy little voice.

"I was holding him and praying for him and he started to shake really a lot, and then he … he kind of … stopped, and then he … arched his back all the way back and just sort of shook … and then he stopped. And he just stopped. And I could feel him in my hands just leave and his life … " A tear races down his cheek. He inhales jaggedly, and the air locks up inside his chest. A moment passes. He stares away, then the exhale escapes, shuddering out of his tiny body. " … he just died. He died in my hands."

"Alex, I am so sorry. Sometimes. Sometimes things die," and I'm thinking, *"Everything* dies."

I continue. "He was a good bird. You were so good to him." Then, "I know he is with God in Heaven," and I'm thinking, "I have *no idea* if he's with God in Heaven."

"Sometimes, we don't get what we pray for," and I'm thinking, "Only *sometimes?*"

It's one o'clock and they've *finally* put a cast on Shawn's arm, all the way up to the elbow. Let's Get Out of Here.

It's a long walk back to the Suburban. I lead the procession, trailed by a rather inappropriately gleeful

Shawn with his colorful new cast, followed by Alex with his coat and his tie and his adorable fuzzy hair, solemnly carrying the little brown cardboard box.

We get in the car.

"What do you want to do?" I ask Alex.

"EAT!!!" says Shawn.

"Shawn, I'm talking to Alex."

Alex says, softly, "We may as well go. We may as well go to the symposium."

So, we drive over to the AFCEA symposium to demonstrate our Block of Wood with Two Wires Sticking Into It and on the way over, Alex works to compose himself, straightens his tie, and even takes a feeble swipe at his orb of fuzzy hair, which instantly poofs back into its usual state of disarray.

We arrive. He's emotionally exhausted but he's determined to do this. He's ready to "Do the Talk and Show the Block."

I open the back of the Suburban and pull out the Award Worthy Display Board and hand it to Shawn's good hand. I pull out the I Don't Understand Electric Motors Report and give it to Alex. I look for the actual project itself, The Block of Wood with Two Wires Sticking Into It. I look in the bag with the assortment of batteries, magnets, and wire. I look in the glove compartment. I look everywhere.

There is no actual project itself, no Block of Wood with Two Wires Sticking Into It.

I shut the back of the Suburban and lean against the door.

Life. Death. God. And the mysteries of science.

It's all too much. Taken together, all at once, it's irresistibly hilarious. I surrender to laughter, sliding down the door until my hands come to rest on my knees, trying to keep my balance.

I take the boys to Rubio's for Fish Tacos.

A few tables over I recognize Dr. Walters, an orthopedic surgeon from Children's Hospital. I wave, he waves, Alex politely waves, and Shawn flails his new cast in delight. After we eat lunch, I send the boys on ahead of me to the Suburban and stop to say hello.

Two years ago, Shawn got a rare and very serious bone infection in his foot, which, it turned out, was overwhelming his immune system and would have killed him. On a Friday evening at about six o'clock, when everybody else was packing it up to go home, Dr. Walters waited around for the lab results and minutes after looking at them, Shawn was rushed into surgery. He spent ten days in the hospital, several weeks in a wheelchair, and many months on crutches. Now, two years later, I go over to thank Dr. Walters again. He saved my boy. He remembers Shawn, smiles and says gently, "Looks like your son is doing real well." At that, I sort of lose it. I really don't mean to sprinkle tears on his tacos, but it really doesn't matter.

Alex's best friend, who just died in his hands, is wrapped in a washcloth in a little brown cardboard box in the back of the Suburban, and is bound for a spiritual destination of very uncertain theological consensus. The Block of Wood with Two Wires Sticking Into It has disappeared and I strongly suspect the cleaning lady threw it out. The time I wasted by forgetting the X-rays may have cost us Petey—so I'll face my Maker on *that* issue when the time comes.

But there is this: I have my boy. I have my boy.

MARCH

Many years ago, on March 1st, my friend Phillip Shaw and I set out to walk from the Pacific Ocean to the Atlantic Ocean. We had both finished High School the previous June.

Phillip and I were free, we thought, having not realized that we had indentured ourselves to our ambition, our ambition to walk across America from coast-to-coast. We called our adventure "USA Expedition."

It seemed that walking across America would bring us a sort of validation. For a young man to take on a challenge that most people would not dream of, to span the country, each step a product of one's own effort and fortitude, would impart a self-confidence early on that would serve us throughout our lives. Adulthood challenges to come would not seem so difficult in comparison. I would be a man who had knocked off a big challenge, right out of the gate.

That was the idea. To start adulthood with a big dream and a big success, one which, with diligence, we would inevitably fulfill, for there is no way to fail to walk across the country if, each day, one makes some steps across it.

So on March 1st, Phillip and I set out from the Pacific Ocean to cross the country. We left with our bare feet in the waters of the Pacific, wearing huge backpacks which were our life-support systems.

By our estimations, twenty miles per day would easily have us to the Atlantic in a hundred-and-fifty days of walking, a total of three thousand miles. Allowing for one day a week to rest, completion by September or so was realistic, and by Christmas was inevitable.

I have always loved to explore small byways and towns, the little places, the forgotten, lost, and abandoned places, the remote places that make up so much of our country. I was excited about the chance to be immersed in such places for weeks and months on end.

We had arranged to stay with some friends the first night, about ten miles from our starting point. We arrived sore and tired, early in the process of getting used to the stresses on our bodies.

Fortunately our hosts had a Jacuzzi, and in the days that followed, Phillip and I spent many long hours in it, soaking up comfort and avoiding our inevitable departure. Phillip had developed some nasty blisters on his feet within the first few miles and this gave us the excuse to hang around. Being stupid young men, we didn't really think much about the fact that the large amount of time spent in the Jacuzzi would make his blisters and feet even softer. For my part, I was delighted that the malady was all Phillip's. I could stride easily about the property, the picture of perfect health, holding forth with our hosts, happily speaking in hushed tones about the state of my poor stricken companion, while the miserable and undoubtedly inferior Mr. Shaw passed his days stumping painfully from lounge chair to Jacuzzi and back.

I think it was the pity I gleefully heaped on him which made him decide to be well. His feet weren't getting any better, we were wasting precious time, and one morning he just decided to pack up, squeeze his feet painfully into his boots, tell me we were leaving, and limp out of there with me shouting our hasty goodbyes behind us. The first mile or so was down a steep hill, and I could see that he was hurting. Whenever I suggested that he consider going back, the determination in his face deepened.

He walked through the pain. That day we walked about eight more miles. It hurt me to see him stump along in such pain, but he was determined to walk and let the blisters heal when they would.

When he could walk no farther that day, he went up to the door of a country house and knocked on the door. I waited down on the road as he explained that we were walking across the country, that his feet were giving out, and asked whether we could pitch our tent in the back yard.

When he returned, he told me, "She said, 'Well, I have two large dogs in the back yard, and they would probably tear you up if you tried to camp back there, so I don't think so.'"

A painful mile or two later, we came upon a large open field with a cluster of oak trees at the far edge of it. We sat on the side of the road, eating canned peaches and tuna, waiting for dusk. When it came, we hopped the barbed-wire fence and, ignoring the "No Trespassing" sign, made our way out to the trees, staying low as we went to keep ourselves out of sight.

We slung our hammocks between the trees and shimmied into our sleeping bags. Within minutes we were asleep. The hammocks had never been used before, so they stretched and after a few hours we both awoke to find ourselves wadded into the low point of the "U" shaped hammocks with our hineys resting on the ground. We got out of our sleeping bags and attempted to remedy the problem by re-tying the end ropes. In so doing, we discovered that there were quite a large number of ants in the area. We produced some bug repellent from one of the backpacks and rubbed it onto the end ropes.

Re-tying the end ropes of the hammocks helped a little, but only a little because the trees were too close to really stretch out the hammocks. In the end, the best we could manage was to be mildly uncomfortable, scrunched into a "U" shape all night long.

We were near the Mexican border, and after several hours of semi-sleep, were fully awakened by the sound of six or eight men speaking loudly in Spanish, making their way north on the dirt road which passed a few yards behind us. As they passed, we couldn't see them or make out what they were saying. We were low-hanging fruit, ripe for the picking, completely defenseless, wadded down in the low point of our hammocks. We lay there in our underwear, tightly cocooned with our arms more or less pinned to our sides inside the small sleeping bags, unable to see or understand the aliens.

All we could do was to lay like silent and motionless human *piñatas* and hope they didn't see us. The voices continued as the men walked past, apparently oblivious to us, and disappeared into the night.

At that moment I realized how very much we were at the mercy of the goodness or ill-will of strangers. Everyone we came into contact with on this trip had the power to do us good or harm.

After a week or so of walking despite the blisters, Phillip's feet improved to the point where I was beginning to have a little trouble keeping up with him, though I could of course not let him realize that, or he would have sweet revenge for all the smirking and pity I had showered on him after that first day.

One day after we had crossed the coastal mountains and were in the desert, a truck pulled up and drove slowly along side of us. A wild-eyed man held up a water jug and, giggling, offered us a drink from the jug, the contents of which were sloshing and wet and running down his arm. We politely declined, having no idea whether the contents of that jug were responsible for his obviously altered state, or whether he was just plain crazy.

On a quiet Sunday afternoon a few days later, we walked through a nearly abandoned small desert town. I was a hundred yards ahead of Phillip, a rarity. As I walked along the sidewalk, a pickup truck abruptly pulled up across the street. Four or five Mexican fellows jumped out of the back, yipping and yelling, and ran directly at me. I turned and faced them, trying to quickly wiggle out of the shoulder straps of my backpack while fumbling for my knife. As they crossed the street the leader pointed and yelled instructions to the others. They grinned like hyenas. None of them looked directly at me.

They all ran past me, clearly a circling maneuver to make me spin around before surrounding me. This bought me the extra fraction of a second I needed to finish freeing myself from my pack. Where was Phillip? I positioned myself so the pack was between me and them, so that I could pick it up and block with it or throw it at them, or they could just take it, and spare me. I was glad that I had thoroughly rehearsed for an attack in the weeks of preparation for USA Expedition. I clenched my knife in my fist, blade side up.

I looked up and saw that the leader's back was to me, his face pressed to the glass of the little restaurant I was standing in front of. He dropped his arms, shrugged, turned to his buddies and, disappointed, said, "Closed." They turned and shuffled past me, nodding to me in friendly greeting, climbed back into the truck, and sped off. I stood there wielding my Buck Knife, backpack at my feet, feeling rattled and very, very stupid.

Phillip had seen all this, and arrived at that moment. He doubled over, giggling uncontrollably. This incident was to prove a readily accessible source of great mirth to Phillip for many days to follow. Whenever we were walking along and Phillip burst out laughing for no apparent reason, I knew it was at my expense.

I suppose it was cathartic for him, since I had nearly gotten him murdered six months before we left on USA

Expedition. We had driven down to Pacific Beach with a bunch of guys to do some girl watching and play arcade games in the Fun Zone.

After a few hours of this, I somehow got into one of those taunting teenage conversations with Phillip, the gist of which was that I was going to drive off and leave him to walk home as a test of his fortitude to walk across the country. The ten or so miles from Pacific Beach to his home in Del Mar was a small distance compared to the whole country, I argued, and despite the fact that it would be getting dark, I pointed out that he didn't have the burden of a backpack and it shouldn't be much of a challenge at all. It turned out to be one of those stupid dares that sometimes get people killed.

Giggling and thinking myself to be quite amusing, I drove off, ditching my good friend Phillip. I had a very pleasant evening at home and when I retired for the evening I fell into blissful, stupid-headed teenage slumber.

A little after midnight, my Dad tapped on my door. "Your friend Phillip is on the phone."

He should have been home hours ago.

I picked up the phone. "Phillip?"

"John. Can you come pick me up?"

"Where are you?"

"I'm at a phone booth in the parking lot at the Torrey Pines Golf Course."

I grinned at the opportunity to work him over a bit: "Hey, you're almost there, buddy, why don't you just walk home?"

"Johnny?"

"Yeah? What."

"You need to come pick me up right away. I'll meet you near the phone booth in the parking lot. And Johnny?"

"Are you okay?"

"Don't ... don't park right at the phone booth. Park a little ways away, out of the light. Don't stop the engine. I have to go." Click.

I jumped in my car and sped down to Torrey Pines. Torrey Pines is a large, remote and undeveloped area of pine forest on the coast highway, along the route that Phillip would take to walk home.

I pulled into the parking lot. The only light was near the phone booth. There was no sign of Phillip. I drove around the empty lot, looking for him outside the perimeter. Nothing. Mystified, I parked a little way away from the booth, as he had asked, and waited. A moment later, there was a tap on the passenger side door. Phillip was crouched next to the car, and stood up into view. I reached over and unlocked the door, and he jumped in.

"Let's-go let's-get-out-of-here."

We drove off. Phillip is normally very calm, but as we drove he began to shake uncontrollably. He didn't speak.

I noticed he had scratches on his face and arms. By the time we pulled into his driveway, he was finally able to speak:

"I was walking along the side of the road by the golf course, and a car pulled up ahead of me and stopped. It looked kinda like a police car. It had spotlights on the sides and a big whip antenna. I just kept walking and I was about to walk past it on the passenger side, when the driver slid over and unlatched the door. I kept walking to go past him. Then he opened the door, got out, and smiled…"

He paused for a moment, then stared deep into the dashboard, seeing the moment again.

"The first thing I noticed was, he didn't have a shirt on. The next thing I noticed was … he didn't have any *pants* on." He chuckled at this, then continued, seeing it. "The last thing I noticed was that he was holding a very, very large *knife*."

"Phillip, I…"

"I just ran past him and kept on running. Then he started his car. I jumped over the guardrail, ran into the bushes, and just crashed through the brush. I couldn't really see where I was going. That's how I got these scratches. He drove past real slowly, shining his spotlight. Then he drove off. But a few minutes later he drove by again. He kept driving past, then turning around and driving past again. Whenever he was gone, I moved toward the phone. I waited in the bushes 'til he'd been gone for about an hour before I came out and called you. Then I went back into the bushes and waited."

"Oh, Phillip … you could have been…"

"I know."

And so I suppose I can forgive Phillip his cathartic joy at watching me try to wiggle out of my backpack in time to take on a Mexican gang, only to see that they were more interested in lunch than in me, as I stood there defenselessly defending my sore scrawny sunburned sorry self.

I think the whole knife element gave the two incidents a joyous commonality in his mind. I had nearly gotten my friend killed. Now he could forevermore summon, on demand, the memory of me as I played superhero to an audience of one.

✳✳✳✳✳

After a stay in Tucson, we departed into hiking trails that laced up and over into Mount Lemmon, the village of Summerhaven, and down into the town of Oracle. From there, we walked the fifty or so miles into Globe, Arizona, a tiny, hardscrabble mining town.

The first evening in Globe, something happened to me which I did not, and do not deserve. I was wandering around town, having a look. I was in an "in-between," mood, not knowing exactly whether I was hungry, or tired, or bored, or happy or sad. I guess the best description of what I was feeling, was empty.

A small crowd was just breaking up from some kind of gathering on the City Hall steps. As I worked my way slowly through the crowd, I felt a tap on my hand. I turned around, looked down, and there stood a tiny little girl, sweet and wide-eyed, looking up at me and smiling. She held up a pamphlet to me. I took it, thanked her, and went to sit on the steps of City Hall to read it.

Of course I knew it would be a religious tract, and being an open-minded person, with time on my hands, I took the time to read it and see what it had to say.

As I sat reading, a man came over and introduced himself to me. His name was William Freeman, "Bill," and he was the pastor of a local church.

He wasted no time in getting to the point with me. He asked about my spiritual condition and specifically, whether I knew what it meant to be a Christian and whether I was in fact a Christian.

I found myself feeling instantly uncomfortable. I felt like a hunted animal. I did not like his direct approach, and I told him so.

Bill didn't seem to mind that at all. It didn't stop him for a moment. He continued to bore into me, into the contents of my soul. He was interested in whether or not Jesus was in there, and nothing else. He was unimpressed by my ambition to walk across the country. He was, frankly, rather bored when I tried to tell him anything about myself, other than my relationship, or lack thereof, with Jesus. He deflected my questions and comments about his town or his life or anything other than questions about Christianity.

He was a man on a mission, and the mission was me. Me and Jesus, Jesus and me. Total, unrelenting focus, which I did not like or appreciate, but I found myself agreeing to meet him the next morning to talk some more.

I did not sleep well, and when I met him the next morning, the first thing Bill said to me was, "John, you need to accept Jesus as your Savior." Not, "Hello," not "Good Morning," not "How are you?" just, Jesus. Jesus, Jesus, Jesus.

I did not like the messenger. I did not like his hair, for instance. I did not like his accent. I did not like his style. But I could not help but find his message irresistible.

That night, lying awake in bed, I considered whether it was in my personal best interest to allow the God of All Creation to come into my life, whether I would permit my self to be saved by the sacrifice of His one and only Son. I worried whether it would affect my trip across the country.

I worried how it might change me, my life, my relationships.

I weighed whether God, all powerful God, should be permitted that singular place in my heart of hearts made especially for a relationship with Him. It was a preposterous wrestling match.

Although Bill had been relentless and focused, even his forcefulness did not compare to the power of God I felt that night.

Here I was, fighting with God. What a ludicrous notion. I laughed out loud, and thought, "What am I thinking? That I will win, and God will lose? That I will somehow eventually overpower God?" There was clearly no contest. If God wanted me, he would have me and I told him so and thanked him. I chuckled a bit to myself, then soon fell instantly, deeply asleep, glad to be on the winning side.

I was baptized the next morning. Before I went under, Bill asked what I was thankful for in my relationship with Jesus Christ. I said, "I thank Him for Life."

I shared my good news with Phillip. "Oh no," he said, "now you're going to be one of those Jesus Freaks."

"I hope so," I said, smiling.

Phillip wanted to get on the road again and I told him to go ahead, I would leave in a few days and catch up with him in New Mexico. I stayed on in Globe, got a Bible, and over several days, learned everything I could from Bill about the Christian faith.

Then it was time for me to leave.

It was a bright, silent early morning in the desert when I set out from Globe, Arizona towards Gallup, New Mexico. I walked alone, my pack on my back, my boots crunching in the desert gravel on the shoulder of the road.

Exhausted, I stopped on the side to rest. I couldn't believe how tired I was. I never tired this easily.

I don't want to say that at that moment, "The Lord spoke to me…" I think He's already called in most of the audibles He's planning on for a while, *and* He's written a rather detailed and specific international bestseller that we can all refer to for guidance.

He didn't come through my ears, but this is the gist of what I "heard" in my mind, loud and clear: "John, everything you are doing, every day, is to glorify you. Now that you follow me, I want you to glorify me, not you. Stop patting yourself on the back. Don't try to make yourself greater. Instead, make My greatness known."

This I did not like to hear, but I couldn't deny it. I walked back into town and spent two more days there, contemplating this message and seeing if there was some way to wiggle out of it before I pulled the plug on all of my USA Expedition efforts.

Bill never, ever suggested that I had to discontinue walking across the country. That, he said, was between the Lord and I.

Finally, after much prayer, consideration, and seeking, I decided, *I* decided, to discontinue the walk and return home, for the Lord to make use of me there.

As I say, I can't pin that decision on God. When people ask me why I didn't finish walking across the country, I can't say, "The Lord told me to stop."

I chose to return. Becoming a Christian was the catalyst, but not the cause. Somehow it seems that life is a combination of God guiding us while at the same time letting us decide.

Poor Phillip was out there walking across the country all alone and since there weren't cell phones, it was several days before he knew that. A week or two after I stopped, he decided to turn back home. I felt badly for him. I still do.

I would love to write at this point that after I returned home, God worked in powerful ways in my life and that I became a saint of the church and a soldier for Christ, but I didn't and I haven't.

At best, I am average in my faith, average in my knowledge of the Bible (in other words, pitiful), average in my church attendance and participation, average in my zeal, average in my behavior, my thoughts, I'm average, average, average.

Honestly, I cannot say that I have fulfilled the direction given to me all those years ago. I have not used the years to glorify God; rather, He has carried me despite my failings.

But as I look back over the years, I also realize that the accumulated effect of even an *average* faith in Christ has resulted in a life that is—despite myself—richer, deeper, more at peace, more filled with joy and security than a bedrock faith in "nothing" could ever have been for me. I have a greater confidence about the challenges of this life because I have a hope and a faith in an eternal life in Heaven. With that confidence of a heavenly eternal life, I worry a little less about this life than I otherwise would. Though I appreciate beauty in the world around me, it reminds me that earthly beauty is nothing compared to the beauty of Heaven that awaits. This earth is just a taste, a sample.

To the extent I am a new creation in Christ[*], it is Christ's slow and patient remodeling work in me, and not a result of some program I've put myself on to elevate my holiness in the eyes of man or my Maker.

---

[*] Therefore, if anyone is in Christ, he is a new creation; the old has gone, the new has come!" 2 Corinthians 5:17 NIV

And so, in little Globe, Arizona, my Christian life began, a new and, despite my immaturity, abundant life which I do not and never will deserve. Thank you, God.

$$*****$$

Now that I am not going to work, I have the time to become more than just "average" in my Christian life. But, do I work to increase my faith or knowledge? Not really. Instead, I sport my new Sears coveralls; the kind retired old guys with time on their hands wear. They look a little like a flight suit. I feel good in them. I spend extra money to get the 100% cotton kind, because I plan to sweat in them a lot. I am going to spend all of March working on the outside of the house, starting with a house Painting Project, to make it what it can and should be.

March 1st

Painting Project

Work Day Number 1

It is a brilliant March morning.

I have not been this awake and refreshed at this early in the morning for a long, long time. Other guys are pulling out of driveways and heading off to work. For me, for now, this is my work.

I stride out into my yard in my new coveralls, master of all I see. I survey the landscape. There is so much to do.

The underside of the eaves are both moldy and pocked with termite damage. When we bought the house ten years ago we had a termite inspection and the report said that the house didn't need to be tented for termites again. I've since learned that virtually every house has at least some termites, so we should have tented anyway.

Instead, the termites have been chomping away at this house unchallenged for ten years plus the seven years our predecessor lived here. Shortly after we moved in, evidence of their diligent efforts began to show under the eaves of the house where the tiny wood castings pushed through pinholes in the paint.

I take a ski pole and push it into a pinhole and the paint membrane rips away as termite castings cascade down my neck and inside my new Sears coveralls.

Splotches of mold grow everywhere under the eaves where the prior owner assured us he had mixed mold inhibitor into the paint he had used.

I drive to the corner of the Home Depot parking lot to select the gentlemen who will be in charge of repainting our home.

I talk with a competent-seeming fellow named José, which is pronounced, "hose·A." We strike a deal.

In Spanglish, he politely suggests that he really thinks I need two people for the job, then agrees with himself:

"I don't know. Maybe is betty chew habba two people. Whatchu theenky? I don't know, maybe is betty. Chess, is betty." He pauses for a moment, considers his wisdom, and staring a bit skyward, nods in agreement with himself. "Is betty. Chew needy habby two people helpy chew. Pour painty."

The conclusion of the matter has been reached.

Then from back in the group of hopeful workers, a less-competent seeming fellow trots out of the audience, looking around like a dazed and lucky gameshow contestant.

"Deese my brother."

"Nice to meet you, what's your name?"

He garbles something unintelligible to the ground.

I ask again. He garbles again. I can't make it out.

I ask José. With a slight wave of his arm, José repeats his brother, sputtering some ancient and guttural phrase. It's not Spanish and it's not a name, it's just what they call him, and it doesn't sound very nice. I give up. I know enough English profanities as it is. I don't need to learn foreign ones as well.

Since I never do get his name, I make one up: José is my main guy, so let his sidekick brother be henceforth known as Hose B.

José and Hose B follow me to my house in their car.

I will have a full day's work for José and Hose B, preparing the house for paint. We'll patch the holes, hose off the mold under the eaves with a solution of water and bleach, and sand lightly. That will take care of the prep phase. Then tomorrow, we'll paint. This will go fast. I think José is right about needy habby two people helpy.

Before we start, I need to finish finding all the termite damage.

The Mexican fellows stand patiently in the shade of the trees to watch me, the shiny-headed middle-aged man in the beige Sears coveralls, walk around the house, poking it in the underside of the eaves with a ski pole, raining termite turds down his neck. They listen to his cries of anguish each time he succeeds. Something odd about these Gringos.

After a while I am satisfied that I have uncovered every pocket of termites and am ready to patch the damage. I want to patch the damage myself, so while I do that, they can spray the mold off the paint with the water and bleach.

I put some bleach in the hose-end sprayer and explain in bad Spanish what I want them to do. Blank stares.

Exasperated, I demonstrate: I turn on the hose full blast and stand underneath the eaves in my coveralls. I blast underneath them pretty hard. Bleached water rains back down on me, softening my skin and getting in my eyes and spotting my new Sears coveralls.

"*Como ese*" I say, which means, "Like that."

Confused looks continue. Fine. I can't really ask these guys to lose their epidermis for my eaves, so I sputter out, "Cut the lawn." I'll just wash the mold off the eaves myself.

My English, they understand. Their shoulders pop up and they gait enthusiastically to the mower, a fine electric mower that a neighbor got rid of when Michael was an infant.

José solemnly takes responsibility for the machine.

Hose B turns it into a two-man job by managing the placement of the extension cord, apparently drawing on some previous *vaquero* job experience. With a ceremonially solemn expression of great self-importance on his face and his whole body countenanced to reflect the skill and gravity associated with his task, Hose B whips the cord needlessly about the lawn in the trail of his mowing brother.

I find my skin diving mask in the garage, put it on, and continue around the perimeter of the house, spraying up under the eaves and getting rained on in result.

The mower stops abruptly.

Now, one would think that if one were employed as a full-time extension cord *vaquero*, if that were the only thing one was occupied with, that one could reasonably be expected to keep the cord from being run over by the lawnmower. For Hose B, alas, such is not the case. I come around the corner of the house to find Hose B holding up the two ends of severed cord in front of his puzzled face, while standing in a puddle left over from my eave spraying efforts, about to unwittingly electrocute himself. I turn and run around the house to the circuit breakers and turn them off before he can succeed. Then I go into the garage and unplug the extension cord.

While I'm repairing it, José and Hose B shuffle in and mutter and look around. I try to explain to Hose B that he could kill himself by standing in a puddle with a live wire, but I drift off the road of my knowledge of Spanish and, based on his horrified expression and my likely misuse of the Spanish words for "kill" and "death," think I unwittingly issue a death threat instead.

I finish repairing the cord and they return to their work.

After I finish spraying, I go inside to shower off the bleach. When I return, the lawn mowing is complete and the two are standing idly in the shade.

I inspect under the eaves and realize that, though the bleach spray did loosen a lot of the mold, there is still remaining mold that has to be wiped off the eaves by hand with a sponge, then rinsed again. I figure I'll just do it myself, so I ask them to sand the loose paint off the front of the house. I set them both up with sanding blocks and sandpaper and they go to work.

By the end of the day, the front of the house has been scraped and sanded for painting and I have cleaned the mold off the underside of the eaves. My fingers are pink where the skin is thinning and peeling from the bleach. I rinse them for a long time under cold water.

Now, all we have to do is sand the eaves—they'll just need a little scuff with the sanding block—then we can begin painting. This place will look so great after it's painted. I'll have Hose B sand the eaves.

March 2nd

Painting Project

Work Day Number 2

Another brilliant March morning. I am in my newly washed jumpsuit from Sears. The shoulders are splotchy from the bleach. It is so great to not have to go into work today.

José and Hose B arrive. José and I will patch and prime the front of the house, which is wood, and Hose B will sand up under the eaves. The sides and back of the house are stucco, and we will do a little stucco repair later on today.

I have a ladder and a sander set up on the side of the house under the eaves. I take Hose B around the side of the house and demonstrate, sanding a section between two rafters. I give all parts of the section a little scuff, then get down to move the ladder to the next section. Elapsed time: 45 seconds.

"*Solo un poquito. No mucho tiempo,*" I say, then in English, "Only a little. Not much time. Just a little scuff."

I set Hose B to the task and return to the front of the house to work with José.

When I return twenty minutes later, Hose B is still working in the section that he started in.

"No, no" I say. "*Solo un poquito.* Just a little scuff."

95

"*Nthee*" says Hose B. Hose B speaks! Hose B speaks in dull, flat, hesitant, nasal monosyllables, so when Hose B says, "*Si*," which means "yes" and is pronounced "See," it comes out like this: "*Nthee*."

As long as he understands: *Solo un poquito*.

I move him and the ladder to the next section of eaves. I say, "*Solo un minuto*."

I watch him work for a while, then say, "Good. Stop. Next." I get him down from the ladder and move him over one section, then send him back up. He climbs up, settles on the top step, gazes dully about as if not quite sure how he got there, and begins to sand. I decide I better watch, but at the same moment realize that I can't bear to watch.

I escape to the front of the house and continue to work with José. José is a great worker. He anticipates what I want to do and is there to do it. He works diligently and effectively and intelligently. More than once, as I've turned to him to ask him for a tool, he's already got it and he's handing it to me.

A few minutes later I hear a yelp. I run back to see what is wrong. Hose B has struck a pocket of termite castings which are pouring out of the eaves and all over him. I turn my head away from him so I can privately enjoy smiling about it.

Katie calls us to lunch. Over tamales, I again explain to Hose B the need to move right along with the sanding work. About one minute per section. He says, "*Nthee.*"

March 3rd

Painting Project

Work Day Number 3

Another brilliant March morning. I am in my jumpsuit from Sears. The shoulders and chest are splotchy from primer. It is so great to not have to go into work today.

José and Hose B arrive. José and I will continue to patch and prime the house, and Hose B will sand under the eaves.

I have a ladder and a sander set up on the side of the house under the eaves. I take Hose B around the side of the house and demonstrate, sanding a section between two rafters.

Then, trying to catch his eye, I add emphatically, "*Trabaja mas rapido hoy*: Work faster today."

"*Nthee.*"

José and I work on the front of the house. We find yet another pocket of termites and dig out the soft and rotten wood. This house is going to take a lot of patchwork. But he and I are getting a lot done. José is a really, really good worker.

I check on Hose B. He has moved to another section. It has been about thirty minutes, and he is on to another section. That's good. I don't know if he is just starting or just finishing that second section. I could try to talk to him and drive myself crazy, I could fire him, likely losing them both, and sand all those eaves myself, or I could just accept my fate. Hose B seems to have accepted his.

March 14th

Painting Project

Work Day Number 14

Today is a big day. Hose B completes the sanding of the eaves. Now we can paint.

Better still, stock in the company I left tumbles 53% today, one of the largest single-day drops of any stock in the history of the S&P 500. (Investigators soon discover that earnings were fraudulently overstated by billions in order to attract investment to build those hundreds of stores, and the Emperor and his minions are sent to Federal Prison. My old boss Roy Prince sidesteps the worst of it and actually keeps his freedom *and* his job, while his boss is sent up to do time. The stock ends up dropping by 90 percent. Am I surprised? No. Do I feel vindicated? *Nthee*.)

March 30th

Painting Project

Work Day Number …. Unknown

The house is finally patched and painted and gorgeous. My beige Sears coveralls and my glasses are completely splattered with paint. Katie seizes upon the condition of my glasses as an opportunity to bring me into the current decade.

*****

"There's no problem with my glasses," I tell her, but she keeps staring at my face. "They're fine!"

"Fine," she says.

"Honey, I mean it. I like them. There's nothing wrong with them … stop staring … *what!?*"

"You got them at the Price Club," she says.

"So? I got a good deal."

"It's called Costco now. It was called Price Club several years ago."

"So my glasses are a few years old, so what?" I ask.

"Late Eighties"

"Well, they look good on me"

"They don't look good anymore."

"How could they not look good any more? They're the same glasses as when I got them."

She sighs and shakes her head as if to say, "Oh, John, there's so much that you will never understand..."

I have a secret. The reason, the *real* reason I do not want to get new glasses, is that I have an *enormous* head. It doesn't *look* like an enormous head, but it really, really is. As long as I refuse to get new glasses, no one will know. I bought the glasses I have because they have huge, oversized frames, which make my Fat Head look smaller in comparison.

I dodge the issue until one day when a slight problem shows up...

Katie and I are in the furniture store. We are helped by an enthusiastic, over-fifty-year-old-lady who's clothing style and hairstyle loudly proclaim, "I'm an over-fifty-year-old-lady with a sense of FLAIR and STYLE!"

"Fine." I think to myself, "Whatever. As long as we can just talk furniture."

She's showing us a coffee table when suddenly she stops and looks right at me.

"You know," she says, "I *really* like your glasses! Nice big frames! They make you look very intelligent."

"Thank you" I answer. I cast my gaze over to Katie, while wearing an intellectually superior expression that says, "A rather nice complement, don't you think so, Honey? Now let's have no more of this silly talk about getting me a new pair of ..."

"Where did you get them?" the lady continues. My wife begins to smile.

"Price Club," I say proudly. "Forty-nine bucks."

"Price Club?"

Katie explains: "Oh, it used to be called Price Club, but that was years ago. Now it's called Costco."

Thank you, Honey.

Surely, the lady is only making conversation, flattering me. She isn't really interested in my glasses.

Uh-oh. She keeps staring. I wish she'd talk about coffee tables some more.

Like a fighter pilot with the enemy on his tail, I drop some chaff: "They have a lot of different styles there. You know, at ... at Costco. But I ... I don't think you can get these there anymore."

Katie smiles just a little more.

"So about that coffee table ..." I continue, turning on the afterburners. But the enthusiastic over-fifty-year-old-lady with a sense of FLAIR and STYLE! has Target Acquisition. It's like "Top Gun."

"I REALLY like them. You know ... "she looks at me quizzically ... " you know, I think ... yes, you do. I know who they remind me of!"

She flips up the trigger guard.

"You really look just like SALLY JESSY RAPHAEL!"

Missile Launched. Target destroyed.

Katie is holding in her giggles by pressing her tongue, hard, up against the inside of her top teeth. She'll save her giggles for later when she can thoroughly enjoy them. Like chocolate.

"I REALLY LIKE them," the lady continues, "I'm going to have to see if I can find some like those." Debris falls to the earth in a wide swath.

I quickly take an enthusiastic interest in all things furniture. I persist and eventually distract her into selling us the coffee table.

Surely that was an isolated incident. I decide to put it behind me. I don't want to be compared to a late 80s talk show hostess.

But a few weeks later, my wife and I are soaking in a Jacuzzi at Donpa's club. A woman in her fifties is in there, too, and she and my wife are conversing. All that's visible of me is my shiny forehead and my foggy glasses. She turns to me and says, "You know, I REALLY like your glasses!"

Although it was a different lady, it was the same conversation, Sally Jessy Raphael and all.

I've discovered that the secret to Fat Head glasses is what I call "The Springy Bow Feature." That means that what I call the "Bow," or the part of the glasses that goes along the side of the head, is attached with a spring-loaded hinge, so my Fat Head can spread the glasses without breaking 'em. Take note.

The good news is that The Springy Bow Feature is almost invisible.

The bad news is that I STILL get those oh-so-attractive grooves in the side of my head where the Bow snuggles into a cellulite canal and makes its own special brew, "Eau de Fat Head."

All this inspires me to write An Poeym:

AN POEYM,
"My Fat Head"
By John Valdez

I'd hoped the world would never know
My glasses have The Springy Bow.
The "Theys" might call me "Mutant Creature"
If They knew I had that Feature.
And yet, my Head and Bow are Pals—
Together, they make sweat canals.
(What's made from glasses squishing hard?
The fragrance, "*Eau de Tete de Lard*.")

I'd hoped the world would never know
My glasses have The Springy Bow...
And yet my Fat Head fame still grew
'Til half the Western States soon knew
I'd won some ribbons here out West
In "Bulbuous-est Head Contests"

I'd hoped the world would never know
My glasses have The Springy Bow
But fame grew more—to say the least—
My Fat Head's now well-known back East:
For Macy's has been after me,
Their promo guy thinks I could be
A Thanksgiving Day Celebrity.
"Inhale some Helium," he said,
"Then float along with your Fat Head.
Through Central Park ... Times Square ... down Fifth.
Your Head will be the Stuff of Myth."

I'd hoped the world would never know
My glasses have The Springy Bow.
But now "They" call me "Mutant Creature"
They know about The Spring Bow Feature.

As I enter the eyeglass shop, I am pleased to notice that there are no other customers. I discretely test each pair of glasses that the clerk offers me to see if it has The Springy Bow Feature. At last, I find a pair with Springy Bows.

"I like these," I say.

"They're only two hundred dollars, on special," the clerk smiles.

"ONLY two hundred dollars?" I tap my finger on the pair I'm wearing. "Mine were only forty-nine bucks at the Price Club!"

"Price Club?"

Never mind. "Why are these so much? Two hundred seems like a lot."

"They're designer frames."

"Well, they look like pretty ordinary frames to me"

"They're Polo, by Ralph Lauren."

"How can you even tell?"

He turns the glasses over and shows me. On each nose pad there is a teensy, weensy, teeny, tiny golden image of a horse with a man riding it, swinging a mallet.

In other words, by putting my nose between two horses and a man with a stick, I'm supposed to feel "special." Two hundred dollars of special. Is this idolatry, or what?

Right then, my wife walks into the shop. She keeps staring at my face. Her pupils widen. Her eyebrow flickers.

"WHAT!?"

"Those look good on you," she smiles.

Sold.

Plus, they have the Springy Bow Feature—that lovely, wonderful, nearly invisible, marvelous, comfortable secret friend—of Fat Headed persons everywhere.

With my new Laurens, I am a hip and groovy young forty something. I join a Literature Discussion Group, filled with hip, young, "with-it" people. I think about how I now look like Ralph Lauren and forget all about Sally Jessy Raphael.

As I sit sharing in the group, a teensy, weensy, teeny tiny screw slowly backs out of my glasses, unbeknownst to *moi*. It lets loose just as I'm comparing the metaphor Emily Dickinson uses in … BOINK! Out comes the screw, BOING! goes the little loop of wire that holds the lens in, only it's not a loop anymore, it's more like the letter "C", then CLINK! out falls my right lens—*wobba-wobba-wobba-wobba-dink*, onto the table.

This is a special moment for me. Although it's good I don't look like Sally Jessy Rafael anymore, I bet *she* doesn't have to carry a teensy weensy screwdriver everywhere she goes…

APRIL

Thursday.

Spring must be here because I saw Donpa rolling down the highway in his red and white "Vee-Dubya," his 'Dub, his shiny two-tone classic Volkswagen Van. Once he's absolutely convinced that spring is here to stay, the "Dubya" comes out of storage.

My station wagon is in the shop and I need to drive downtown tomorrow — Friday — to pick up materials for the church growth drive. I have to borrow Donpa's 'Dub.

When I ask Don if I can borrow his van, it's obvious that he isn't comfortable parting with it. He can't exactly say, "no" — family and all, but he sure seems to wish he could. I'm pretty sure Donpa likes his van better than he likes me. After a long and unenthusiastic discussion, he slowly hands me the keys. I make a mental note to be sure to return the van fueled and detailed.

About Donpa and me: He's a little intimidating. He's my high school girlfriend's father. He's the guy with the big biceps. I'm the little dude who dated and married his lovely daughter, Katie. He holds a Ph.D. in theoretical physics, speaks five languages and, of course, loves Shakespeare. I speak bad English (English badly?), have forgotten my Spanish, and love Bugs Bunny.

In honor of Donpa's love of Shakespeare, I wrote this little play about how I had to ask to borrow his van:

DONPA'S 'DUB

ACT I
[Scene I – The Palace]

Enter SIR DONPA *and* VALDEZ, *a footman*
VALDEZ "I beseech thee, Don, to use thy van
  And promise thee the utmost care I can."
  (Don clutcheth in his hand the sacred key
  And sizeth up the worth, or lack, of me.)
DONPA "Oh. Lo, low Juan, err, John, ahem, aha."
  [*Aside*] "I thinketh how this catcheth in my craw.
  Was not my daughter Katie quite enough?
  Perhaps I'll tell this footman, 'Sorry. Tough.'
  Through decades I've endured enough already
  Starting when he asked her to go steady.
  Then fortnights later, Kate, Valdez spoke of
  And paired these words together: 'Kate' and 'Love.'
  Now he dareth paireth words like 'Dub' and 'key'?
  In truth, this Valdez fellow's buggin' me."
    [SIR DONPA *hesitates, hands keys to* VALDEZ]
  "Take leave, you have my blessing," saith he.
  (Not.)
  "You've keys to all the best that I have got.
  Just bring her back here to me, safe and sound.
  Try not to burn my 'Dubya' to the ground."
NARRATOR
  Valdez then bows to leave, and with great flair
  He turns and well nigh runs away from there.

End of Scene I

Friday. Dawn.

I awaken long before the alarm, bristling with ideas, energy, belief, and possibilities. I jump out of bed while it's still dark, eager to get downtown and pick up The Jesus Video Project materials for our church growth drive.

"Where are you going," Katie mumbles, half asleep.

"To get the *JESUS* video stuff for the church. Let's all go out tomorrow as a family and visit the houses."

"We can't."

"Why not?"

"We're going out of town this weekend, remember?"

"Oh yeah. Well, then, let's go with the kids after they get out of school today."

Silence.

"Okay?" I ask.

"What about Alex's concert?" she asks.

"Oh," I say, learning anew that Alex must have a band concert at school tonight. "It's at seven, right?"

"I'm not sure. I'll check after I get up."

"I think we'll have plenty of time, Kate."

"Are you sure?"

"Katie," I chuckle, "you worry too much." I feel wonderful today. I feel … unstoppable. Katie rolls over and goes back to sleep.

I cook, devour and clean up a big, manly breakfast. I open the garage door — the sun is just coming up. I back

Donpa's 'Dub carefully out of the garage. I turn out of our street and onto the freeway frontage road, happy to be on my way.

Attendance at our small traditional Protestant church hovers at around sixty people, week after week, year after year. The people and programs are solid and excellent, though the church building is a little bit hard to find. The church is well-funded and its members are very devoted, yet we just never seem to grow. It has been very frustrating.

Everyone at church is excited to get started on The Jesus Video Project. It's an excellent tool for church growth, and I'm excited to do my part to grow the church.

The *JESUS* video is a full-length motion picture about the life of Jesus, based on the book of Luke in the Bible. It has proven to be a very useful tool for missionaries the world over to teach people about Jesus, people who are very often hearing about him for the first time.

The Jesus Video Project is pretty straightforward: The neighborhood around the church is divided up on a map, and everyone at church is given a street or two to cover. The Program itself takes place on three successive weekends:

Week One, as a family, we go to the houses on those streets and ask people if they'd like us to bring them the *JESUS* video, for free, on the following week. If no one is home, we leave a little flyer, which they can use to request the video by check-marking a box on the flyer and leaving it by the front door.

Week Two, as a family, we deliver the videos to those who have requested one. Then, we ask if we can return in a week to see what they think of the movie.

Week Three, we return and try to answer any questions the person might have. We offer them a brochure about the movie and, if they wish, we lead them in a little prayer accepting Jesus Christ as their Savior, becoming Christians. Cool! It's simple, effective, and only a three week commitment. Great for church growth.

I rumble along the frontage road in Donpa's 'Dub, climbing a steep hill. I hum happily.

I check myself in the rear view mirror:

Hair: Perfect

Eyes: Bright and eager.

Collar of New Shirt: Perfect

I feel like a tiger, but Donpa's 'Dub is losing power as I charge up the hill. I downshift.

I take a closer look into the mirror:

Teeth: Perfect

Smoke: Pouring out back of van.

The van rolls to a stop, the engine sputtering. I set the parking brake and leave it in neutral so I can see why it's running rough. I know quite a bit about cars, and expect to have this little problem cleared up and be on my way, still arriving first thing this morning. Nothing can stop the Valdez.

I open the engine hatch on the back of the van. Fresh air rushes in...

Hawumpf!

Flames. Real ones. Several of them.

My car's on fire. Well, not really my car, Donpa's. Donpa's 'Dub. Donpa's precious red and white shiny two-tone classic Vee-Dubya Van.

I start screaming, "My car's on fire! My car's on fire!" as if that will do anything. The flames continue about the business of igniting the engine, ignoring my screams, as unflustered, businesslike, and delighted as a bunch of raccoons.

I open the car door and, wild-eyed, check to see if there's anything I should get out of there. Fortunately there is nothing worth saving but my skin.

A car is coming—Hallelujah! The driver carefully eases himself past me and my problem while I wave my arms and jump around, my screams nicely muffled by his closed windows.

A moment later another car pulls up and stops. Answer to prayer! A benevolent looking, middle-aged Hispanic man, with an assured, confident countenance gets out of the car. He's holding a fire extinguisher! My Guardian Angel! All will be well, I can see it in his face.

He clenches his teeth, pulls the pin, and lines up the nozzle. This unpleasant bit of business will soon be over, I'll get the oil leak repaired, be on my way, and still beat all the traffic.

Like some kind of subtitled Schwarzenneger, he strafes the engine compartment with the fire extinguisher. *"Hasta la vista*, baby."

"Pshht! Pshht! Pshht!" the extinguisher hisses. I'm sure that's gotta feel really, really good.

Did you know that Volkswagen Vans have magnesium engines? I didn't know that. Once magnesium catches fire...

One Thousand, One.

One Thousand, Two.

One Thousand, Three.

HAWUMPF!! The engine re-ignites. Once magnesium catches fire, it burns so hot it can't be put out. I didn't know that either. Flames shoot enthusiastically out the engine compartment.

The Good Samaritan's grip slips and the extinguisher clinks emptily to the ground.

His shoulders slump, his head drops. He trudges back to his car, climbs in, and wordlessly drives off, a broken man, leaving the spent extinguisher behind.

Let's review:

It's early, so Donpa is still fast asleep, but if at this moment, he were to think of his coveted 'Dub, he would think of the fine oblong bus, pretty as a poundcake, washed, waxed, fueled and gleaming, fire engine red — make that candy apple red — and snow white. Beautiful.

What I'm looking at in the same dawn's early light is a roiling, broiling hulk, well on its way to becoming fully engulfed.

Isn't it interesting how very different two peoples' perspectives can be on the same thing?

Further, when Donpa thinks of me, he thinks (I hope) of his mighty son-in-law, good and kind, capable, doing good things in and for the world each day. I ponder this as the heat of his burning van warms me in the morning chill, and as the smudgy oil smoke darkens my new white shirt to a sooty, odd-looking, ashen-gray tone.

The fire starts to crawl underneath the vehicle. Now, there are a couple of things under a vehicle that behave interestingly when they burn…

I hear the fire truck coming. Maybe, just maybe, if they get here now and react really quickly, they'll be able to save it. The siren is getting louder. I move up behind the van to get a damage assessment, to see if there really is any hope.

...parking brake cables, for example. The parking brake cables underneath a vehicle behave very interestingly when they burn. This happens now as I stand behind the van, which is in neutral with the parking brakes on, at the top of a steep hill. The cables burn through, the parking brakes release, and the flaming backside of Donpa's beloved 'Dub rumbles randomly downhill at ever increasing speed.

I turn and run for my life. The vehicle steers itself at whimsy—no real pattern, though in a generally downhill fashion. Believe me, I prefer to stand like a matador and let the bull speed past while I wave my cape—*Ole'*—as it goes, but there's no way to tell which way it's going to swerve next, or how it's going to come to a stop.

The only thing at all predictably Newtonian about its behavior is that it is picking up speed as it rushes down hill.

Before it can mow me down, though, it swerves randomly and goes off the side of the frontage road, down the embankment, and crashes into the fence along the freeway. The van and I are each at the perfect viewing angle for early morning freeway driving entertainment. Me, panting with hands on knees and gasping for air, Donpa's 'Dub spectacularly aflame.

The van then ignites a brushfire along the side of the freeway. Drivers slow down to watch, slipping past,

116

sadistic secret smug smiles, sipping their coffees, enjoying the spectacle of the burning van and the frantic, middle-aged Accountant or Lutheran or Mormon-looking guy in the rumpled gray dress shirt.

The firemen arrive and spring into action, a well-trained team. I cheer them on. Maybe they can save it, they might just save it. Hoses come out. Big equipment, large shiny valves, reflective yellow suits, thick boots — excellent for tromping — make loud scuffing noises. I am impressed.

They rush toward the van with their fire hose.

No. They rush right *past* the van with their fire hose.

Then they spray the brushfire alongside the freeway, ignoring the van. It must be some kind of endangered freeway-side brush. Our tax dollars at work.

"WHAT ARE YOU *DOING*?" I scream. The Captain tells me they use chemical fire extinguishers, not water, to put out car fires and sure enough, a moment later, more firemen rush up to the van with nice, big, manly, industrial-sized fire extinguishers and, just like action movie heroes, blast away at the flames in the engine compartment. *"Hasta la vista, baby."*

PSHHT! PSHHT! PSHHT! PSHHT!

Count with me now, won't you?

One Thousand, One.

One Thousand, Two.

One Thousand, Three.

HAWUMPF!! The entire back end of the van re-ignites, exactly as it was, followed shortly thereafter by the sound of several industrial-sized clonks on the ground, and the retreating, tromping scuff of thick firemen boots.

I think of Donpa. I wonder what he's doing.

The fire resumes its work underneath the vehicle.

Besides parking brake cables, the other thing under a vehicle that behaves interestingly when burned, is a gas tank.

I would love to write that a gas tank on fire is as spectacular as it is in the movies because it would make a better story, though I'm actually glad it's not, because I would be dead. But when that baby blows — and it does — the fireball satisfactorily puts to rest any lingering hopes of salvaging Donpa's 'Dub.

The van burns and burns and burns for half an hour, despite the firemen keeping a continuous blast of water aimed at it. Finally, after the last drop of gasoline burns away, both fire and firemen call it quits.

As the firemen pack up to leave, I stand beside the warm, ticking, charred remains of Donpa's 'Dub. He's probably awake by now, adjusting the feathers in his cap or something. Here's how it goes:

[Scene II - The Palace]

Early morning. SIR DONPA *awakens*

DONPA "Alas, I've had a most disturbing dream!
I'm wondering what ever could it mean:
A twenty-foot-long loaf of bread in flame?
And standing nearby, helpless, … what's-his-name.
'Tis clearer now — a van — or roast marshmallow?
And watching it, that sooty Valdez fellow.
This cannot be! No, never! Not my 'Dub!
This dream will pass, soon as my eyes I rub.
But nonetheless, this morning I'll call John
Right after I have put my codpiece on."

NARRATOR But 'ere Don made the call, John called him first.
The news the footman gave him was the worst:

[Scene III - VALDEZ, on telephone]

VALDEZ Good morning Sir, how are you? How you been?
Uh, listen, can we talk, just friend to friend?
I'm calling you … I'm sure you wonder why…
First, may I warmly compliment your tie?
She's fine, she's fine. The kid's are healthy, too.
But something's up, it has to do with you.
I really wish that this was all a joke
But, Donpa, gosh, your van went up in smoke.
Uh-huh, Yessir, oh, sure. I understand.
Click!
That didn't go exactly as I planned…
[Curtains]

Friday. 5:14 p.m.

After dealing with Donpa's Demolished 'Dub, renting a car and picking up the videos, I stumble, exhausted and hungry, through the door. Katie says, "Alex's band concert is at six."

Here are the instructions for the first week of The Jesus Video Project:

The Jesus Video Project
Instructions
WEEK ONE: AS A FAMILY, visit the residences assigned on your map. Saturday afternoons are best, but avoid Friday and Sunday afternoons. Introduce yourselves and your church, and ask if they would like you to drop off a free video on the life of Jesus in the coming week. (If no one answers, you may leave a door hanger which explains how they can mark the check box and put it outside to receive the free video.)

Here's how "Week One" of The Jesus Video Project *actually* goes:

Friday Evening, 5:23 p.m.

While the kids stay home to wolf down dinner, I dash from house to house leaving the little door hangers with the check-box for people to mark. No time to ring the doorbells, introduce myself, or ask it they would like a free video.

I finish and zip off to Santa Fe Christian, only slightly late for Alex's band concert.

Here are the instructions for the second week of The Jesus Video Project:

> *The Jesus Video Project*
> *Instructions*
> WEEK TWO: TAKE THE VIDEO *to the home of the respondent with a bag of microwave popcorn, saying, "We hope you enjoy both the video and the popcorn." Ask if you can return in a week to find out what they thought of the video.*

Here's how "Week Two" of The Jesus Video Project *actually* goes:

It's Saturday morning and we are all getting ready to pile into the station wagon—which is back from the shop—and go hand out *JESUS* videos to whoever wants them, along with a little flyer.

"Shawn," I say, "get in the car. Do you have your shoes? Find your shoes. We're going now."

"Where?"

"To do the videos."

"What videos?"

"The *JESUS* videos. The ones I handed the flyer out for last week."

"Do I have to come?" Shawn asks.

"Do I?" Alex chimes in, hopeful.

"How-bout-me-can-I-go-to-Jason's" drones Michael.

"I want to go to Emily's" Vanessa interjects neatly.

"No, kids, we're all going. Get in the car."

"What's the movie about?" someone asks.

"Jesus."

"Jesus?"

"The life of Jesus, based on the gospel of Luke in the Bible."

"Is it any good?" someone asks.

"Yes. It's good. It's … actually, I'm not sure I've seen it. Kate, did we see it back in college?"

"I don't know."

I look at the clock. "We have to go. Get in the car right now."

"But Dad…"

"JUST GET IN THE CAR RIGHT NOW, Shawn!"

"But Dad…"

"Enough. I don't want to hear any more! JUST GET IN!"

We drive back to the neighborhood where I've handed out the flyer. It's an unseasonably warm April day. "All right, everybody, we'll pray and then we'll get out of the car." I pray for the success of the Project, then say, "Let's go."

"Dad?"

"What, Shawn."

"I think the sidewalk might be too hot for my feet."

"So wear your shoes."

"I don't have any."

"Why not?"

"I was looking for them, but you told me to just get in the car."

"Why didn't you tell me anyway?"

"I tried to, but you said, 'Enough, I don't want to hear any more,' and to 'just get in."

"Okay, Shawn, you'll just have to stay off the sidewalks and try to walk on the lawns and in the shade. Sorry."

"That's okay, Dad."

Because I'd run out of time last week, there are no "respondents." However, we know they have the door hanger. With our big, smiling, normal happy family, everyone who we talk to seems to suspect that we are from some kind of a cult. We manage to foist off perhaps five *JESUS* videos.

On the drive home, I spontaneously pull into the parking lot of a nice little restaurant. I'm going to take us all to lunch. "C'mon," I say, "let's go have a nice lunch."

"Dad?"

"Yeah, Shawn."

"What about that sign?" He points:

```
┌─────────────────────┐
│                     │
│     NO SHIRT        │
│                     │
│     NO SHOES        │
│                     │
│     NO SERVICE      │
│                     │
└─────────────────────┘
```

Shawn doesn't have any shoes, so we go home.

I take a long, long nap.

Here are the instructions for the third week of The Jesus Video Project:

The Jesus Video Project
Instructions
WEEK THREE: VISIT THE RESPONDENTS, asking if the video was enjoyed and if there are any questions. For the respondents who prayed the prayer to receive Christ at the end of the video, leave a Gospel of Luke for them to read and make an appointment to return the following week with Lesson One of the Basic Bible Studies.

Here's how "Week Three" of The Jesus Video Project *actually* goes:

Saturday a.m.

"Okay, kids, everybody come in the living room so we can watch this movie."

"What movie?"

"The *JESUS* movie. I figure we ought to at least watch it before we go out and ask people what they thought of it."

We sit down to watch it, and it turns out to be an authentic, beautifully made film, biblically based on the Gospel of Luke. It is a powerful presentation of the birth, life, crucifixion, resurrection and ascension of Jesus. At the end of the movie the narrator says,

"The tomb, in which the body of the Lord Jesus was placed, is empty. Three days after his crucifixion, he rose from the dead. He is alive. He wants to come into your life. Jesus himself said, 'I am the resurrection and the life. He that believeth in me, though he were dead, yet shall he live.'

Almost two thousand years have passed since Jesus rose from the dead. And he still lives today as the greatest and the most powerful influence in the world. The proud statesmen of the past centuries have come and gone: rulers, scholars, scientists, philosophers and theologians have come and gone. But Jesus still lives today.

He is the most unique person who has ever lived.

His birth was unique. The Bible tells us he was born of the Virgin Mary.

His life was unique. His life was characterized by the supernatural. He lived a holy life without sin, and performed greater miracles than anyone who ever lived.

His message was unique. He offers love, forgiveness, and a new way of life to all who receive him as Savior and Lord.

Wherever his message has gone, new life, new hope, and new purpose for living have resulted.

His death on the cross was unique. Two thousand years ago, the God of the universe sent his only son, Jesus Christ, to be the sacrifice for the sin of all men.

He died for you.

His resurrection was unique. Three days after his death the most amazing event in history took place: Jesus rose from the dead.

His birth, his life, his death and his resurrection all prove that Jesus is exactly who he claimed to be: The Son of God, the Savior of all mankind. This same Jesus Christ is alive today.

He wants to come into your life, forgive your sins, and give you the power to live an abundant life. Listen to his words. 'Come unto me all you that labor and are heavy laden, and I will give you rest. I am the way, the truth, and the life. No man cometh unto the Father but by me.'

The Bible says, 'For all have sinned, and come short of the glory of God.'

It also says, "The wages of sin is death, but the gift of God is eternal life through Jesus Christ our Lord."

When Jesus died, he paid the penalty for your sin. Right now he stands ready to come into your life. 'Behold, I stand at the door and knock. If any man hear my voice and open the door, I will come into him.'

To experience his love and forgiveness and receive eternal life, you must receive him as God's sacrifice for your sin, and invite him to come into your life by faith.

If this is the desire of your heart, you can pray a prayer of faith and Jesus Christ will come into your life.

This is a suggested prayer. I will say it first.
'Lord Jesus, I need you.
Thank you for dying on the cross for my sin.
I open the door of my life
and receive you as my Savior and Lord.
Take control of my life.
Make me the kind of person you want me to be.
Amen.'

If this prayer expresses the desire of your heart, pray this prayer right now, where you are. Pray after me silently, as I repeat it, one phrase at a time.

'Lord Jesus, I need you.

Thank you for dying on the cross for my sins.

I open the door of my life

and receive you as my Savior and Lord.

Take control of my life.

Make me the kind of person you want me to be.

Amen.'

Now that you have prayed this prayer of faith, and invited Jesus Christ to come into your life, you can be sure that he came in, because he promised he would, if only you would ask him.

You can also be sure that your sins are forgiven, that you are a child of God, and have eternal life.

If you want to experience the full and abundant life which Jesus promised, talk with him every day in prayer. Discover his wonderful plan for your life by reading the scriptures. And meet with others who love and follow him.

Finally, remember always his wonderful promises: 'I will never leave you or forsake you. Lo, I am with you always, even unto the end of the world.'"

Wow. I had no idea we were handing out such powerful stuff! What if these people we're giving these movies to were ever to see our family as we really *are?*

"Okay, kids," I say, "let's go. C'mon, we need to hurry." We pile into the station wagon and return one more time to visit the neighborhood. We had passed out five videos the prior week. This week, three of those people are at home.

At the first house, a young woman answers. We ask her if she has had a chance to see the movie.

"Yes."

"What did you think of it?"

"It was good."

"Did you have any questions?"

"No."

"Did you have a chance to see the whole thing?"

"Yes."

"Did you see the part at the end, where the Narrator comes on?"

"No."

"Would you like a pamphlet?"

She smiles politely while closing the door, "I'm a Catholic," she explains. The door closes.

At the second house there are a half dozen or more young children playing. Two are in the yard and a third is crawling out a garage window. Inside are two more kids. A big friendly man with a large mustache and a ready smile answers the door. Katie recognizes him as Dr. Brad Wilson, a prominent local chiropractor. His wife Tracy invites us in and introduces herself. She and Brad introduce their six children. She is pregnant with number seven. She offers us lunch.

Brad tells us they "mostly" watched the movie, it was great, and they've seen it before. Tracy beams at Brad. I notice that she beams at Brad a lot. Brad asks us about our church and tells us they attend Calvary Chapel. Brad pulls out his wallet and insistently gives us $20 to apply toward the cost of The Jesus Video Project.

Sheepishly, we accept the contribution but decline the offer of lunch. Tracy waves goodbye, our kids say goodbye and we leave. When we're outside I say to Katie, "I feel bad about not staying for lunch."

"John," she says, "fourteen people for lunch and she's about 11 months pregnant? You've got to be kidding."

An older gentlemen answers the door at the third house. His name is Jack Kellogg. Behind him, at the back of the house, his wife sits hunched in profile, silhouetted against the drawn curtain. Jack is friendly and cordial, but hasn't seen the movie. He asks what church we are from and when we tell him, he lights up. "Isn't Ernie Robbins the Pastor there?" he asks. "I've known Ernie for years and years. I'd love to get down there and come visit your church…" He stops, and turns a grave eye back into the house. "My wife is pretty sick right now. I can't really do it. I have to be with her."

We wish him well and head back to the car. I confess I am a little disappointed. I wanted to be better missionaries. Aren't I supposed to "glorify God, not me? … not try to make myself greater, instead make God's greatness known?" I've done little or none of this since Globe, Arizona, and now, as I try to fulfill God's purpose for me, I fail spectacularly. No takers. I'm sad to have done such a poor job at my most important job…

Epilogue 1

While the kids are getting in the car, I decide to actually read the pamphlet that we were supposed to give out this week. Katie asks me to read it aloud. It says,

> *"The film, JESUS is the most watched and translated film in history. Millions have responded to His message of hope and love.*
>
> *To experience his love and forgiveness and receive eternal life, you must receive him as God's sacrifice for your sin, and invite him to come into your life by faith.*
>
> *If this is the desire of you heart, you can pray a prayer of faith and Jesus Christ will come into your life.*
>
> *This is a suggested prayer:*
>
> *'Lord Jesus, I need you. Thank you for dying on the cross for my sin. I open the door of my life and receive you as my Savior and Lord. Take control of my life. Make me the kind of person you want me to be. Amen.'*

If this prayer expresses the desire of your heart, pray this prayer right now, where you are."

"Wow." I say.

"That's strong stuff," she adds.

At that moment, a tiny voice from the back of the station wagon says, "I would like to pray that prayer." A moment later, another one says, "Me, too."

Epilogue 2

Jack Kellogg came to church a few weeks following the distribution of the *JESUS* video. His wife had passed away. He's been attending Grace Church ever since, he says, because a kind family came to his door and invited him.

Epilogue 3

It took Donpa a long, long time to recover from the loss of his beloved 'Dub, but I knew he finally had a humorous perspective on the whole incident when I opened my birthday card from him. Tucked inside it was the charred DMV Owner's Certificate for his beloved 'Dub, which he'd somehow salvaged from the glove box. On the part of the Certificate used to transfer ownership, he had filled in my name.

"No matter what the lowly footman says,
Loaneth not thy van to John Valdez."
— Donpa

MAY

I am going to expand my horizons in May.

For instance, I'd like to learn how to order a beverage at Starbucks. I know that I like either Mochas or Lattes, but I can never remember which. And that's just the basic stuff.

The more advanced Starbucks terms give me classroom flashbacks. Advanced Starbucks sounds like terms from Sociology 502, or Boolean Algebra: The Venti Paradox, the Whip/No Whip-Guilt/No Guilt Decision Matrix, and the entire Shots Enigma. My eyes glaze over. I flashback and see the professor, chalk clacking away on the board as he scribbles things I do not recognize, my jaw hanging, his jaws moving, the sound fading in and out like the Omaha Beach landing scene from "Saving Private Ryan."

Besides knowing *what* to say, there is a *sequence* to say it in; a syntax, a grammar. Like French. And like French, you'd better not butcher it when talking to the natives.

Fortunately, Katie is completely fluent in Starbucks. I always go with her and she does all the talking.

But today is different. Today, I decide to go to Starbucks by myself and order something to drink. A really big day for me.

I drive up the Coast Highway from Leucadia to Carlsbad. The view of the beach north of Leucadia is stunning. I'm feeling Grand. Did you ever have one of those days, or one of those moments, when you feel that the whole world is just laid out there before you, for the taking? I feel like Teddy Roosevelt. Bully. Me, Starbucks, you know. Sure, I go there. I order stuff, you know.

Though the parking lot is a little small, I angle my head upwards like I am clenching a fine Cuban cigar in my teeth and I drive confidently on. I am the master of all I see. My wheel smacks the curb and I drive up over it and onto the planter, mortally wounding a sprinkler. In my battle to keep my "Grand" feeling, I blurt out "I meant to do that," and saying that actually helps.

I stride into Starbucks and survey the scene. Do you ever wonder what these people *do* for a living? Here it is, 8:45 on a Monday morning, and *everyone* is so shabby-chic, so well-to-do, so masters of all *they* see. Moreover, they look used to feeling that way *all the time*. It's obvious they aren't anyone's employee. And self-employed people work more hours than employed people. So, I conclude that everyone here is a GSU. "Gainfully Self-Unemployed." There's no place they absolutely *have to* be either now, or really, ever. On paper, depending on the Dow, they gotta be up into the six … seven … eight figure category. How did this happen? I mean, some of these GSU's were too young to vote in the last election. I go to the counter. I'm a little nervous. I do hope I get this right. I think I like Mochas. Or is it Grandes? I mean Lattes. My wife would know. Mochas. Okay, I'm ready. It's my turn now and I take a breath, and in a surprisingly self-assured voice, I hear myself say, "DECAF MOCHA GRANDE." The cashier calls out "DECAF *GRANDE MOCHA*." (Did you hear how he switched the last two words and emphasized them for my benefit?) I'm not going to give up this Grand Feeling, this Teddy Roosevelt with a Fine Cuban Cigar, this "Bully" Feeling, this Expansive Feeling. Even if I'm still working on the grammar. I settle comfortably at my table and take in the morning sun, looking informed and studious with my *Wall Street Journal*. I am the master of all I…

Hey, wouldja just get a *look* at that guy at the next table? He's everything you would think a GSU. would be. I nickname him Trent. He inspires me to write this Poeym:

For "Trent"
AN POEYM,
"GSU, 'n Tight"
By John Valdez

I'm a righteous GSU
I see myself, I don't see you

Just leave me to my uptight bubble
And there won't be any trouble

Through all stoplights, watch me zing
While Uptight-Skinny-Man-Bike-Ride-Ing

I'm young and rich, you wonder how?
Let's just say I watch the Dow.

I'm in Love, you want to see?
Here's an eight-by-ten. Of me.

My beard is short, my body's lean
From CNN and straight caffeine.

"So-Cool-Beneath-My-Baseball-Cap"
(The fact is, I'm about to snap...)

My order comes: "Grande Latte?" the Starbucks guy calls out. I cradle my *Wall Street Journal*, stride up to the counter, pick up my coffee, stir in ¾ packet of Sugar In The Raw, and settle among the GSU's into the comfort of my chair. I am proudly self-nurturing every fiber of my hedonistic being. Ah, it's My Turn. (Somewhere, my Guardian Angel starts to giggle...)

I relax and drink deeply. I am master of ... hmmm, it's not quite as sweet as when my wife orders it ... hmmm. Then I hear, "Decaf Grande Mocha? *This* is *yours*." The counter person looks at me. I've taken someone else's cup.

There is a ripple as everybody in the place simultaneously realizes that I've taken Trent's order. He looks desperately around the place for some kind of emotional support, as if to say, "Didja *see* that? Can ya *believe* it?" Well, everyone *has* seen it and no one *can* believe it. Trent receives waves of deep and profound sympathetic understanding. As the crowd recovers, an after-ripple flows through the place, a slow shaking of heads, a "tsk, tsk, tsk," a certain, "Well, I suppose this sort of thing was *bound* to happen. I mean, haven't you been *watching* that guy?" Newspapers go up over faces. I choose to believe that everyone in the place is an accomplished speed reader, inasmuch as their heads all swing from side to side.

Trent, for his part, doesn't say anything. He doesn't scream and yell. But with his eyes clamped shut and his head shaking back and forth, in disgust, he emits intermittent puffs of pneumatic pressure throughout his sinuses, scowling. This offense was beyond words. To complete the effect, I have a robust cough that day and have amply contaminated his coveted Latte. I, John Valdez, am the Schmoe who wrecked Trent's day with my guzzling, slobbering, coughing affront, okay? Apologies are offered, confession is made, but forgiveness of sin (from Trent, anyway) is out of the question.

I am surprised by what happens next. My embarrassment begins to evaporate and the warmth and goodness, even grandness of the day begins to rekindle itself. I assess the situation. Well, I have *my* order. *And* his. And it tastes pretty good. I might even like these Lattes better than those Mochas. Thanks, Trent. The sun is shining. Life is still good. I settle into my chair.

The corner of Trent's mouth twitches.

He's at the next table, about to pop, fitfully flipping the paper, shaking his head and desperately trying to put his day back together while he waits for his order to be made all over again. To my surprise, I find myself settling more deeply into my chair, relaxing, and peaking at him from behind my *Wall Street Journal*. Expressive, intermittent high-pressure leaks continue to plague Trent's sinuses. I take another sip. I hide behind the paper because, I'm sorry, Trent, but I just can't stop smiling.

✱✱✱✱✱

It's Thursday and I am sitting with Katie on the little balcony at the Pannikin in Leucadia, overlooking the Coast Highway.

We've perched our helmets on the extra chairs at the table. Downstairs, near the front lawn of the Pannikin, we watch as people walk in and out of the door, casting looks of curiosity, amusement, admiration, and nostalgia to our tiny bike.

When I was twelve, the youngest of three brothers, I dreamed of and hoped for a Honda CT-70 minibike. I remember laying on the bottom bunk and looking up at the slightly torn gauze under the top bunk with my hands cupped behind my head, elbows spread out, wakeful, hopeful, thinking.

My brother had passed a Honda CT-70 four-color catalog along to our Dad that day. The word was, "Dad was thinking about it," though I couldn't directly verify this from Dad without being pounded by my brothers.

The CT-70 is the ultimate minibike. It is distinguished by a huge crossbar which makes it look like an oversized sewing machine. It has three speeds, an automatic clutch, headlight, horn, and even an ignition key. This is a bike for a twelve-year-old teenager to *go* places. *Important* places. (Though technically, none of that "going" would be exactly legal.)

In those days, other minibikes had lawnmower engines, tubular steel frames, belt drives and only one speed. There was no horn or any neat gadgets, and starting them was an undignified lawnmower pull-start affair.

With Dads, of course, it doesn't have to be Christmastime. Dads get to do what they want to do, when they want to do it, and sure enough, one bright Saturday morning, Dad told us boys to get in the truck. As we bunched together on the silver-gray vinyl bench seat of Dad's '67 El Camino, we were the most polite pack of squished brothers ever to overlap vehicular airspace. Two hours later, we rolled home with it: a brand new 1971 golden yellow Honda CT-70, the finest machine ever built. It stood upright and dignified in the bed of the truck, head held high and proud, like the Best of Breed of a somewhat unusual pedigree.

Riding the CT-70, I experienced, for the first time, power over a piece of equipment which in itself had power —a wonderful feeling until I panicked and ran into the fence in the back yard and the bike started to climb up the fence and I fell off and it fell over on me and the engine whined and the tire spun in the air and Dad reached down, smiling, and shut it off. My Dad had the best attitude about this. He was always, well, pleased with our little mishaps, as long as we weren't really hurt, seeming to prefer that we accumulate our lifetime allocation of crashes early in life, and at relatively low speed.

Over time, I learned how to ride the minibike better and better, and became comfortably in control of it. Eventually, there may even have been the odd cop-dodging trip to the Seven-Eleven for licorice whips, though my brothers swore me to secrecy on pain of death by Dutch Rub, so I won't say for sure.

When I was sixteen, I got a job at "King's Grill." It was a little walkup fast food counter on Santa Fe Drive, behind the Shell station. The owner, a Korean gentleman named Chun Bin Yim, "Mr. Yim," called it "King's Grirr" and as a smart-aleck teenager, I gleefully called it "King's Grirr," too. He was the most hard driving and frugal man I have ever met. That was many years ago, but when I drive into the wealthy community of Rancho Santa Fe, I notice that there is a big house on the left with the nameplate "Yim" on it, and I wonder.

The minibike was too small to ride all the way to King's Grirr, so we traded it in for "something bigger." That was the end of the little Honda CT-70 and the end of all that went with it, and worse, it was the end of simple, joyful, cheap transportation.

Decades passed and my own three little boys came along.

Then, one day we saw an advertisement for barely-used Honda CT-70s at a dealership out in El Centro, a desert town about 100 miles from home. My boys and I drove out "just to look," I told them. We found a whole fleet of tiny gleaming bright red Honda CT-70s lined up in the showroom. I was twelve again, and sold. Although the bikes were five years old — the last year they made them — one of them had only eight-point-one miles on it and was in perfect condition. Beautiful. The manufacturer had long since replaced the gobs of chrome on our 1971 model with loads of plastic on the newer models, but I was pleased nonetheless. Automatic clutch. Headlight. Horn. Ignition key, and even a place to mount a license plate. Ahhh.

I stood there just like my Dad and watched three little boys fall in love with a Honda CT-70.

Each of them, with eye contact, enthusiastically and earnestly pledged to provide free lifetime minibike maintenance. A short time later, we loaded our nearly new, bright red Honda CT-70 into the back of the Suburban.

On the drive home, my boys bounced off the inside of the Suburban, brimming with reverence, loyalty and excitement over the bike, yet having never actually ridden a Honda CT-70. I pulled off the interstate and found a little area for them to try it out.

By the time the odometer had reached eight-point-seven miles, the minibike was missing three of its four turn signals and the headlight was staring up and off into space, catatonic. Nevertheless, I was pleased. Pleased that my kids considered a 70 cc minibike to be a big machine; pleased that their falls stung but didn't maim; pleased that they'd learned that motorized stuff can get out of control. My father taught me well.

I suppose my boys will grow up and want "something bigger" some day.

But just because my kids are going to grow up doesn't mean *I* have to, and so I have returned to my childhood appreciation of semi street-legal activities.

When I ride my minibike I feel twelve again, zipping through the neighborhood, leaning forward, the engine whining, top speed of about 27, dreaming once again of outrunning and outsmarting the "fuzz," taking the secret route that cuts through Glen's back yard and the vacant lot and the dirt road and then through the bougainvillea tunnel, disappearing without a trace, leaving the cops in awe while I laugh like Peter Pan in my secret hideout.

And sometimes, like today, Katie and I ride it down to the Pannikin and park it near the front lawn where we can watch former little boys admire the Honda CT-70 minibike, once again.

*****

I have to write about my grownup motorcycle. I know, I know, people hate to have other people tell about their motorcycle.

It's in our genes to hate hearing about these things. Eons ago in the cradle of civilization, nomads huddled around campfires to drink yak butter tea and talk about camels. The women would sit off to one side, weave, and get annoyed at all of this camel talk, the flames reflecting in their glaring eyes.

Finally, one of them would sigh and mutter, *"Ha'ang chon chun,"* meaning, "I do NOT want to hear that camel story again."

Then one of the men would angrily cut her off, *"HAH! SIY!"* An awkward silence would follow, then talk among the men about the wonders of the camel would slowly resume and there would be a fragile peace in the camp.

Generations passed. Those nomads are gone but their genes are still with us.

Along comes Roy Rogers and his horse, "Trigger." No one wants to hear about the wonders of Trigger, or so one would think, but there is actually a museum where

Triggephiles from the world over come to see the stuffed remains of the Great Steed himself.

That being the case, I figure I can write about my close friend and motorcycle, my Yamaha TW200, my "Bikey." No muttering. *HAH! SIY!*

I'm going on a 125 mile ride across the desert with a group of backcountry motorcycle riders.

The group requires that each bike be licensed for the street because the route includes a few short sections on the highway. In order to be licensed, a motorcycle has to have turn signals, headlight, and a rear view mirror.

I'm slow. I start early so that as many riders as possible can pass me, and therefore see me, along the way. That way, if I break down, someone might have a better idea where to look for my remains.

For the first few miles, I hit every obstacle I see. Every rock, every rut, every sand pit. I careen from one obstacle to the next, my legs sticking out the side like a rodeo cowboy's. The other riders whiz past me, ignoring all this stuff that I seem to be finding so important. Don't they even look at those obstacles?

Then I try ignoring the obstacles, too, and only allow myself to look where I want the bike to go. It works. The bike seems to just sort of float along the visual path I trace with my eyes. I wonder if Roy Rogers had that kind of connection with Trigger.

I hit a patch of sand and carefully slow down to a safe speed, muscling the bike through it to stay in control.

For improved safety and visibility, the turn signals on my bike are oversized and stick out to the side on long rubberized stalks. This makes the turn signals easier for others to see, and I'm so much safer in highway traffic. To me, they're what a motorcycle turn signal should be.

Not so for these guys: a turn signal on their bikes is about the size of a nickel, and it's stuck flat onto the side of the fender.

With my wide-angle rearview mirrors, I can see everything behind me.

These guys' rearview mirrors are about the size of a dental mirror, and they use zip ties to lash them down out of their way onto the handlebar. Even if they *did* have nice rearview mirrors such as I have, these are not rear view mirror kind of people. They would never, ever look in them. These riders just go straight forward, flat out.

And there's none of this "muscling" through the patches of sand. They simply hit the throttle, skip over it, and forget about it. After a while, I start learning to do the same.

The size of my bike's engine is about 200cc. Most of these guys have 400cc bikes or bigger. For me, if I can reach 50 mph, it's a good day. For them, 50 mph comes and goes in under four seconds. Their bikes can cruise at over a hundred miles an hour all day long.

Were I my own ancestor, telling of the wonders of my camel, the other camel guys would get up for yak butter tea refills in the middle of my story...

HAH! SIY!

By mid-afternoon, everyone in the group has passed me and the route has become much more difficult. I am alone, checking my map at the bottom of Mormon Canyon, a cobblestone-filled, rock-walled ravine that climbs steeply up from the desert floor to the top of a high mountain plateau. "We gotta go through *THERE?*" I ask nobody as I sit in absolute desert silence. I look at the map, I look at the mountain, and I can't see how I'm ever going to get up and through. But I have no choice. There is no "sweep" vehicle and I am all alone. I ride into the canyon. It's scorching hot. I bounce and scrape along, kicking up rocks, smacking boulders, and trying to keep power on the throttle. After a short section the canyon turns and a whole new section presents itself, just as troublesome as the prior section. I ride through the next section. Then the next. I try not to think about the whole mountain, just ride through each small section before me.

BOOM! I hit a boulder and drop the bike on its side with the back tire spinning and the engine whining, moaning like a wounded, well ... camel. I reach down and shut off the engine, putting it out of its misery. Then I lift the bike up, climb on, and restart the engine. We ride through another difficult section. I fall again and the bike goes over on its side. I notice that my left boot is wet with some kind of fluid. Probably gasoline, because a motorcycle will leak gas when it's on its side. I ride another section of the canyon. The gasoline on my boot doesn't evaporate. I rub it with my glove. It's not gas. It's oil. I've popped a hole in my engine case, which could strand me out here, but I can't stop now to check it, just a little further and I'll be out of this canyon and up on top of the plateau where I can patch the hole with some bonding material in my tool bag.

After making it to the top, dribbling oil all the way, I get out my repair kit, mix the bonding material and push it into the hole. I have to wait about fifteen minutes for the bonding material to cure.

All this "bonding" with my bike inspires me:

AN POEYM,
"Ode to My Bikey" (#1)
By John Valdez

No one likes my Yamaha
They just say, "Yeah … gee … mmm" and "huh"
None want me to serenade
About the trip my Bikey made:

We hit a boulder, it went "WHAMMO!"
(You couldn't do that on a camel.)
Bleeding oil, wounded thing,
Laying there in that ravine,
My Bikey rose, and with such care
It got my hiney out of there!
Now I love my bike so dearly —
But that's not what you want to hear-ly.
Sure, you're happy I'm not dead —
You liked what you've already read…

Oh my Bikey … could be bigger…
But my Bikey is my "Trigger."
Oh my Bikey, how I love it.
My wife says, "If that's true, then stuff it."
That angers Bikey, hands on hips,
It starts to cry through trembling lips,
"If that's the way it's going to be
You'll have to choose: It's her, or me."
Bikey's forced my hand, of course
I guess I should have bought a horse…

151

After 125 miles across the desert, I pull into the hotel parking lot. A Jacuzzi and a steak sound pretty good. I shut off my bike, peel off my helmet, and enjoy the silence. After I have a shower and a long soak, then put on clean clothes and my Ugg boots, we all go out for steak. I know I'll sleep tonight. After dinner, all the riders gather by the fireplace in the lobby to relax and begin to talk about their motorcycles…

I know, I know. *"Ha'ang chon chun."*

*****

Friday.

I have a lovely wife, and four beautiful children who are growing up so quickly, and I am the most fortunate man alive to be able to spend some real time with them, without the constant worry about making a living.

Right now, today, before I get too involved in the next phase of working on the house, there is a tiny opening to spend time with my sons. I decide to start with Michael, the oldest, and take him out to the desert to camp and go minibike riding.

This will be one of those father-son outings that I could never have pulled off before. I know a lot of Dads who have the energy to work long hours all week, then load up the camper on Fridays and head for the desert, or pack the kids in the car and go to a theme park.

I am not one of those fathers. Every Friday for as long as I have been working, all I can remember wanting to do is to rest and recover from the monstrous week I have just had. But now, such is not the case. I am going to take Michael, my fourteen-year-old, to the desert. There we will have "The Talk," though Katie tells me I am way too late. Well, that may be, but I will give him "The Talk" anyway because it's my job to do so, even if I have neglected it until now.

We pack up my Bikey and the CT-70 and head out to McCain Valley. I have a book for him, and a Promise Keeper's ring. He, of course, does not know that I intend to ambush him with these items.

McCain Valley is a beautiful, barren, isolated area about two hours drive from home. We arrive in the afternoon and after setting up camp, we have enough daylight left to zip around, discovering little trails off the beaten path and wending far, far into the backcountry.

I follow Michael when we make our way back to camp. He goes around a corner and suddenly confronts a rather steep and bumpy four foot drop off. He doesn't see it in time. Rather than lace his way through it, he bounces down it, hitting every large rock on the way. He flies over the handlebars, the minibike soars into the air, then plummets down onto him. I laugh, stop my bike, and help him up. He complains about his foot hurting. I tell him to walk it off.

We have steak for dinner. He keeps his foot in a bucket of ice. After dinner I sit, uncomfortably, wondering when, how, and if to begin "The Talk." I say, "The Talk," as if there is some specific speech I have to give. I honestly have no idea what I'm going to say. I'll just let Michael lead...

For some reason, all campgrounds are located in places where, the minute the sun sets, it gets cold. Really, really cold. Well, the sun sets, it gets really, really, cold, and I decide to just get a good night's sleep. We're tired. His foot hurts. We can deal with this "Talk" business in the morning.

It's dawn. Michael wants to go riding. Though I am hungry for breakfast, I only have a glass of juice to save time. I figure we'll just go for our ride and then come back and eat.

Off we go. Michael says his foot hurts. Even though I am on my Bikey, which is bigger and more powerful than the CT-70, I have trouble keeping up with him. He's a good rider. We are lacing through trails that curve back and forth in a series of "esses." The trail goes through thick vegetation, and it is impossible to tell if anyone is coming from the opposite direction.

I am a little bit concerned. I don't think Michael is aware of the risk of a head-on collision.

We get to an open area and stop. I give him the lecture about oncoming bikes, how one has to be careful, and one must be prepared for an over-fast and out of control rider coming through the bushes the other way. He seems to understand. Then I ask him if he'd like me to demonstrate how to turn on a berm.

A berm is a mound of dirt that gets pushed up on the outside of a turn, making for a banked turn. A good rider can use the bank, or the berm, to his advantage to get through a turn very quickly.

Never mind that my son is going through the turns more quickly than I am—the old man just wants to show the lad a thing or two.

Michael, I say, "Ride over to that berm so you can see how I do this."

Michael reaches down, lifts up the foot shifter with his hand, and clicks the minibike into first gear.

"Michael, why are you shifting with your hand?"

"My foot hurts."

"Oh ... well, let me show you this."

I decide that I will slowly show him how to ride the berm so he can see what I do and hear me as I talk him through it. I ride into the corner and go high up the side of the berm, then turn the handlebars, swing the bike over, and gun the throttle to come down the face of the berm, which is about three or four feet high.

When my front tire reaches the flat ground at the bottom of the berm, I can't control the bike, I just cannot control it.

"Now, I have ridden motorcycles for many years," I tell myself in that nanosecond, "and I know how to control this bike." I muscle it, I fight it, the front tire hits sand and digs in. The handlebars clock all the way to the right. I try to hang on, but the bike has come to a complete stop, whereas I haven't. Yet.

I sail over the handlebars and land on my left shoulder. It makes a loud crunching sound. Okay, I've come to a complete stop now.

Pain shoots through my left side. I roll onto my back and the sound of further crunching noises accompany my moan.

My shoulder feels broken — very, very broken. There is no one around but Michael. I try to sit up, but my shoulder stays on the ground, making crunching, popping, clicking, tearing noises. I'm hurt. I am *really* hurt. I can't get up without my shoulder coming undone.

"Mikey," I say, "you have to go and get help." I am laying on my back, looking up at the sky. "Bring help. I can't get up."

"Which way is the camp?" I lift my head and point off to the east.

He starts the CT-70, reaches down, and clicks it into gear. As he leaves, I yell for him, but he can't hear me. He speeds off, reaches down, and pops it into second gear. To the west. Camp is east.

I have figured out what I will tell my son when I give him "The Talk." It won't be about the birds and the bees at all. Instead, I lay on my back and compose "The Talk" as everything I want him to know regarding this moment as I suffer while he rides frantically the wrong way, searching for civilization while yet plunging deeper and deeper into the wilderness.

JOHN VALDEZ

For Michael
AN POEYM
"The Talk"
By John Valdez

I don't want to wreck my shoulder.
I know this now that I am older.

But even if I do my best
Yet wreck my shoulder, don't drive west.

There's nothing west. The camp is east.
I'll make a tasty buzzard feast.

Go east, my son, get help for Dad.
That crunchy-shouldered Dad you had.

This trip ain't goin' quite as planned,
You're shifting gears with your left hand.

Your bike sailed up in to the air
And landed on your footy, square.

I laughed and took it all in fun,
And said, "Don't be a sissy, Son."

And now my fate is in your hands
As you explore uncharted lands.

My thanks to you would be profound,
If, son, you'd please just turn around…

My son drives up. *"Couldn't-really-find-anybody."*

"Well, son, that's because you went the wrong way." I point up over my head to the trail that goes back to camp. "Take that trail."

"Oh. Sorry."

"No problem."

He hurries off. I get a glimpse of him over my head as he leans forward, reaches down, puts the foot shifter into second gear, and disappears at high speed down the overgrown, curvy, narrow trail, defenseless to any oncoming riders.

A long time passes. This is not good. I have no idea if my son has made it back to camp.

Then I hear a lovely sound: "Whump-whump-whump-whump." I look up and see a Search and Rescue helicopter coming over the ridge. I lay there and wave, stupidly, with my good arm.

The chopper lands in a patch of dirt and they come and get me. They ask me, "What have you had to eat today?"

I say, "A glass of orange juice."

I am airlifted out of there, and a few minutes later, set down in a meadow near the campground, where an ambulance is waiting. I am impressed to the point of embarrassment. Michael has certainly outdone himself.

Some guy offers to retrieve my Bikey, pack up our gear and my son and drive all of our stuff to the hospital. I don't know this man. I explain that I hate to do this, but I ask him for his identification. I figure an honorable man will understand and be happy to prove who he is. I am flat on my back in the ambulance, trying to run things the best I can. He shows me his drivers license and his business card. I write everything down. He says he is a law enforcement officer in the Naval Reserve. His wife pops into the ambulance. She looks normal. I ask her his middle name. I ask what he does for a living. It matches.

The ambulance attendant asks, "What have you had to eat today?"

I say, "A glass of orange juice."

"When?"

"A little after sunrise."

They say, "Would you like some morphine?"

"No," I reply. "I would like some Tylenol."

I call my wife from a cell phone in the ambulance. It goes like this:

"Hi, honey," I say.

"Hi."

"How are you doing?" I ask.

"Good."

"How are the kids?"

"Fine." There is a long pause. "What's up? Why are you calling?"

"Well, I had a little tumble. On the bike. I'm fine, but I thought it would be a good idea to have a doctor take a look at it today."

"Where are you?"

"Oh, I'm heading in now to see what the doctor has to say."

"Are you in the car?"

"Uhh." (I can say, "Uhh" and make it sound a lot like "Yeah." But technically, it's not "Yeah," so I'm really not lying.) "Uhh. I'm heading in now. I thought now would be a good time."

"Are you driving?"

"Uhh."

"What?" she asks.

"*What* what?" I ask back.

"John, who's driving?"

"Can you hold on for a minute?" I cover the phone. "Excuse me, sir, mister ambulance driver, what's your name?"

"Bob."

"Bob," I say into the phone, then, "Do you mind meeting me at the doctor's office? I might be a little too sore to drive home."

"Which doctor? Who is Bob?"

"Uhh." I cover the phone. "Which hospital are we going to?"

"Grossmont."

I uncover the phone. "Bob is the guy who is driving me in, in to see the doctor."

"John?"

"Yes?"

"Are you in an ambulance?"

"What do you mean by 'ambulance'?"

"Does it have flashing lights on the roof?"

"Nope. They are not flashing."

"Where are they taking you?"

"Grossmont Hospital."

Twenty minutes later, we arrive at Grossmont. I have a nice little IV in me, but I still don't get that Tylenol from the medics in the ambulance.

They wheel me in. The nurse asks, "What have you had to eat today?"

"A glass of orange juice." I am offered morphine. I decline, and request Tylenol instead. The pain reliever hospitals use most.

"Sure, no problem," the nurse says.

I lay there for an hour, waiting for Tylenol. Then I'm offered morphine.

"Can I have Tylenol instead?"

"Sure, let me get you some. When's the last time you ate?"

I lay there another hour. A nurse explains that they are "backed up" today.

Ten minutes later a nurse asks me if I need anything. I ask for some Tylenol. She asks if I would like something stronger. "No," I say, "I would just like some Tylenol, please."

My son arrives, hopping on one foot into the ward. A nurse snaps at him, "Don't you hop in here."

A doctor, a real doctor, comes up to my gurney. He asks me if I'd like morphine. "No," I say, "but I would like some Tylenol." This doesn't seem to register. He examines me and then wanders off, mumbling something about getting an X-ray. I want Tylenol. After all, it's the pain reliever hospitals use most. Just not this one. Apparently.

An hour passes. I am wheeled into X-ray and told to hop onto the table. I have to go to the bathroom so badly, I could burst.

I ask the attendant to please bring me a bottle. When I stand up, my shoulder crunches and pops and drops three or four inches. I stand in the X-ray room, filling the bottle and shaking in pain. I am running out of reserves. I am hungry. I am in pain. I am fed up.

When I lay on my back on the X-ray table I reach over with my opposite arm and push things around to reassemble the pieces in my shoulder so it doesn't hurt so badly. I say to him, "Mr. Technician, I have put my shoulder back together, but if you think the X-ray will show more, I am willing—even though it will hurt like crazy—to re-disassemble it for your picture. Do you think the radiologist will prefer that view?" The technician steps behind the screen. "Hold still," he says. BZZZT! Whatever.

I am wheeled back to the ward. The doctor comes to my bedside and says, "We're going to transfer you. We've looked at your X-rays, and this is something we're not equipped to handle. You need an orthopedist."

"Well, what is it?"

"Well, you've damaged your left shoulder and we need to get you to a shoulder specialist."

"Is it broken?"

"We're transferring you to Scripps La Jolla. Would you like some morphine?"

What he's really saying is, "I have no idea what I'm doing." I can't disagree with that, and the sooner I get out of here, the better.

I turn and look him square in the eye. With utmost deliberateness I say, "What I would really, really like, is some Tylenol."

He nods his head with deep understanding, then looks me in the eye and says, "I'm sorry. We can't give you Tylenol because we don't want anything in your stomach when you get to Scripps. Now if you had asked earlier...."

Two hours pass. The ambulance shows up to transfer me to Scripps.

They load me in. "What have you had to eat today?"

"A glass of orange juice. Right after sunrise."

The ambulance driver gets lost going to Scripps. I know the city pretty well from my work in real estate. Though I am laying on my back, I can tell when they miss the 52 freeway.

"You missed the 52, didn't you?" I ask.

"We're on our way to Scripps," they say. Oh.

I feel them get off the freeway to turn around to get back on the 52.

"You're turning around to get back on the 52, aren't you?"

"We'll be there shortly. You just keep comfortable, all right?"

"Now you're going down the onramp onto the 52, aren't you?"

"How does that shoulder feel?"

"We're on the 52 now, aren't we? Can you tell me if we're on the 52?"

Pause. Silence. The question hangs out there, then, "Yes."

I feast on the warm rush of feeling validated for the first time today.

I am wheeled out of the ambulance toward the emergency room door. It's shortly before sunset. I see Katie. Someone asks, "What have you had to eat today?"

"A glass of orange juice. Shortly after sunrise. Can I get some Tylenol?"

No answer.

There is no doctor. The nurse explains that there is no orthopedist in the emergency room, but that the one who is "on call" is on his way.

I'm laying on the cot and the nurse is talking to me when the Doctor walks into the room, tells me his name, and extends his hand for me to shake. I don't catch his name because the nurse is talking.

"I'm sorry," I say, "I didn't get your name." His hand is hanging out there, unmet. I reach out to shake his hand, but I am a little late. He pulls it back, huffs, shakes his head, leans over me, and shouts, as though I'm deaf, *"I said my name is Doctor Ross."*

"How do you do?" I ask, and extend my good hand again.

He shakes it abruptly and says, "Y'know, I just I think you've got a little bit of a chip on your shoulder. I really don't need this attitude from you."

"John…" Katie says, lightly chastening.

"What?"

"Just try to be nice."

"I am trying to be nice. Dr. Ross, I am trying to be nice, but I am tired. I am hurt. I am hungry. I really don't know ... maybe we can start again."

"Maybe you *should*. I think *you* should," he says.

"Thanks for coming in on your day off. I appreciate it."

"That's my job. No problem." Then he says, "You've got a grade 3 or 4 AC separation in your shoulder. No broken bones. I'll give you a shot of cortisone and send you home. Nurse, let's take out that IV" He looks at me, shakes his head and rolls his eyes.

He stabs the needle deep into my shoulder joint and pushes down the plunger. It hurts like crazy. He insists that I sit up so that he can move the shoulder around. My shoulder pops out again then crunches and pops while he moves it in a big circle. I am weeping. He says, "Don't be a sissy."

He puts a brace and a sling on it and tells me to call his office on Monday to schedule a follow up visit.

Katie drives us home. "I'm hungry," I say.

"What have you had to eat today?"

"A glass of orange juice," I look at the clock, "fifteen hours ago."

"What do you want to eat?"

"I don't care. Anything. I have to eat something right now."

She pulls off the freeway and into a small shopping center. Everything appears to be closed, but we spot some people moving inside the Chinese restaurant.

"Chinese," I say. "I want Chinese food. See if they have anything left they can serve us."

Katie goes up and taps on the door. They unlock. They talk. She goes inside.

Fifteen minutes later she comes out with a bag of Chinese food. "Thirty-six dollars," she mutters as she climbs into the car.

We get home. She tells me to wait on the couch while she makes up a plate for me. I lay on the couch. She puts the kettle on to boil water for Chinese tea. (It is not only the *watched* pot that never boils.) I am ravenous. I could eat the stuffing out of the couch cushions.

I ask for a plate of food.

She says, "Don't you want to wait for tea?"

"No," I say. "I am starving. I need to eat something *right now!*"

"Don't get testy. You're yelling!"

"I am not testy. I am hungry. I have to *EAT SOMETHING! NOW!*" Well, okay, now she's right. I am testy. I am yelling.

She looks at me and freezes, wide-eyed. Nothing moves. The whole "NOW" approach I've been advocating is indefinitely on hold. I pull myself up and stumble into the kitchen and my shoulder clunks and makes a crunching sound and drops three inches and I rip open the drawer and grab a spoon and I tear open the little white tub of food and plunge my spoon in and I lean over it and make caveman noises and devour it all down non-stop and it is both the worst Chinese food and the best Chinese food that I have ever tasted.

A week or so passes during which everything is about me, well, at least as much as I can manage to make it so— and I begin to recover. I'm almost off the Vicodin. I'm alert and awake more often. On my first fully alert afternoon, I am laying on the couch when Mikey comes through the door after school, hops uncomplainingly past me on one foot, and thumps his way down the hall to his room.

"Katie," I call from the couch. "That boy of ours is still hopping on one foot."

"I guess you're right."

"Why don't you get it x-rayed? It's been a week."

"I will. I guess I've been so busy taking care of you."

"I appreciate that, but he should be walking. Does he complain?"

"Not really."

"Mikey," I call.

He hops dutifully out to the family room. Thumpa-Thumpa-Thumpa.

"*Yeah-Dad?*"

"How is your foot feeling?"

"*Fine-I-guess. Doesn't-really-hurt-that-bad.*"

"But you're still hopping."

"*Well-it-kindahurts.*"

"Mom's going to take you for X-Rays."

"*NO!*"

"Why not?"

"*I-don't-see-why.*"

"Well, son, it's been a week…"

"*Little-more…*"

"Right. It's been a little more than a week, and you are still hopping on one foot. That's why."

"*I'm-pretty-much-used-to-it … not-so-bad.*"

"Apparently you are used to it. I apologize that we've neglected you the last week while I've been getting all the attention."

"*That's-okay-dad.*"

"You're getting an X-ray."

"*Jeez!*"

"We don't say, 'Jeez,' Son."

I am laying on the couch when the door flies open. Katie and Mikey have just returned from the doctor.

Mikey stumps in on crutches with a cast on his leg. Katie follows him in and says, "Broken in three places."

I have new X-rays taken for my follow-up visit. Doctor Ross examines the X-rays, then invites me over to the board to have a close look. He's feeling grand today. "It's healing very well," he points out. "See how it's healing where you broke it here, and here, and over here?" I can see that the breaks are long, severe, obvious and everywhere.

"I thought I didn't break it."

He turns and faces me, slack jawed and expressionless, taps his knuckle to the X-ray, staring blankly at me all the while. He will not dignify my apparent inability to see the obvious with another single word.

There is no point pushing the question. I'm not going to get anywhere with this guy. Instead of saying, "Gee, Doc, that sure explains all the crunching sound when you moved my shoulder around, doesn't it?" I look at the X-ray and comment, "It looks like this bone here is split lengthwise. Can that be?"

"It is, and you can see here where these tendrils of new boney growth are beginning to fill it in where the bone is split. Remarkable, isn't it?" He smiles.

"Yes, Doctor Ross. Remarkable."

JUNE

It's June. It's been a year since the last one. It's time. I can always tell.

Katie and I are walking down the aisle in the grocery store. I am on her left. As we reach the end of the aisle to make the left-hand "U" turn, she cuts the corner, forcing me in my shoulder sling into the canned peas. I have to stop 'til she passes, then catch up. She continues on her way, oblivious to the fact that I am now two steps behind her. By the time I catch up, she is ready to make a right turn at the end of the next aisle. When she makes her right hand turn, she is unaware that, because I am on the left side, the outside of the turn, I will have to take an extra step or two in order to keep pace with her. As we exit the corner, she is an oblivious length-and-a-half ahead of me. Again I catch up. We pull up to the checkout.

They say you can tell a lot about a person by what is in their grocery cart. Well, I can't tell a thing from ours. This is no diet that I recognize, just a random selection of items from about the store. Plus chocolate. We get out to the car and I unlock the driver's door for her, and let her in. Then I go back to the trunk and load the groceries with one arm. I put the cart away. I walk back to the car and pull on the passenger door handle. Still locked. Katie is inside, staring out the front windshield. I tap on the glass and motion that I would like her to unlock the door. A little frown, a little rolling of the eyes, then she hits the unlock button. As I climb in, she says, "Can't you use your key?"

It's June. It's been a year. It's time for her mammogram. For weeks now, she hasn't made eye contact and finishes sentences with words like "the." For example, "John, would you ... bring me ... the ..."

I am going to be very glad when her mammogram is over. She does this every year and every year she's always just fine. Katie is the most naturally healthy person I know.

When Katie was a little girl, her Grandmother came to Southern California to live near Katie and her family. Grandma Irene had just gotten divorced after nearly forty years of marriage and now, in her late fifties, was starting her life anew. She rented a small apartment downtown and got a job as a night nurse at one of the hospitals nearby.

She and little Katie were very close, and on Sundays they would go to church and downtown to the museums to admire art exhibits. Katie's interest in art started with Grandma Irene.

Late one night, Katie's parents got a call from the hospital where Grandma Irene worked. She had had a seizure. She had not told anyone about the lump in her breast, which had grown to the size of a grapefruit. Cancer had spread throughout her body and into her brain and triggered the seizure.

Grandma moved in with Katie's family, and home became a hospice to her dying Grandmother.

As a little girl, Katie was there to see the good days, and the not-so-good days, the shuttling in and out of friends, priests, and family, to hear the quiet murmurings behind closed doors.

One day, Grandpa and a priest arrived. Grandma Irene stood bravely on unsteady legs, clutching Grandpa, while the priest pronounced them man and wife once again in Katie's living room.

Grandpa left a few days later, and a few days after that, the priest arrived again to give Grandma her last rites. Grandma Irene died when she was fifty-eight. Katie was ten.

When Katie and I were married and away at college, her mother, Margaret, found a lump in her breast. The needle biopsy showed that it was cancer.

But the more we learned, the more confident we became that Margaret was going to be all right. She was able to have a "lumpectomy" rather than a mastectomy, which studies at the time showed led to a similar survival rate. The tumor was small and when it was removed, came out easily and was fully encapsulated in a single, simple lump. Small radioactive capsules were later implanted near the surgical site, chemotherapy followed, and she was deemed "well."

We finished college and moved to Leucadia.

Five years after finding the lump, Margaret began to have pain in her joints and bones. The cancer had returned and spread into her skeleton and liver. Margaret was convinced that the needle biopsy she'd had years prior had unleashed an otherwise harmlessly encapsulated cancer tumor into her system. In other words, the needle biopsy she'd had was killing her.

The doctors started her on a newly-approved medication, which had shown some promise of shrinking cancers and killing them. It was the latest potential wonder drug, and I was banking on it. Margaret didn't improve at first, but I figured good things take time, and if she could hold on, this drug would rescue her.

About this time, an envelope arrived from my brother. Inside was a letter to Margaret with a note on it asking us to forward the letter if we felt it was appropriate.

Here is what the letter said,

> Margaret,
>
> I know that things are not well, and that you may not make it through this time. Dear Lady, may I be bold? Not my words, but Jesus' words? In the New Testament, in the book of John, chapter eleven, verse 25 through 27:
>
> Jesus said to her, 'I am the resurrection and the life. He who believes in me will live, even though he dies; and whoever lives and believes in me will never die. Do you believe this?'
>
> 'Yes, Lord,' she told him, 'I believe that you are the Christ, the Son of God, who was to come into the world.'
>
> I pray that you will do this now, whether God chooses to heal you now or not, for some day each of us must die, and when we do, God wants us to be together with him in Heaven.
>
> Love,
> Freddy (John's Bro)

Well, Katie and I were a little embarrassed when we read that. It was a bit much. A bit intense, a bit presumptuous. It was not really our place, or our business, to get into spiritual matters with Margaret. It wasn't Freddy's place either. But as we looked at the letter we realized that the words mostly weren't Freddy's. Besides, although it wasn't our place to get into spiritual matters, surely it wasn't our place to block them, either. Katie took the letter with us when we went over to visit Margaret and Donpa.

That afternoon, when Donpa and I were outside shooting baskets, Katie emerged from the house, came gently up to me and said, quietly, "Will you come inside?"

As we walked in, Katie explained that she had read the letter to Margaret, and Margaret said, "I want that. That's what I want to do."

We went into the house. Her eyes were clear, her voice was strong, her mind was sharp. We prayed and hugged and wept. After a while she became very tired and asked to sleep. She let me stay by her bedside for a short time as she fell asleep. I prayed and wept and smiled, and after a time, got up, put my hand on her head and whispered, "God loves you, and so do I." She sighed deeply. "I'll see you soon," I said, and closed the door.

She was worse the next day, semi-comatose but clear minded enough to know that she didn't want to go to the hospital, because she knew once she did, she would never come home again. I remember watching her hesitate and resist as she was helped into the car.

A short time after being admitted, she fell into a coma. I thought she would come out. I was banking on that wonder drug to kick in.

I did not recognize how serious it was until I walked into the hospital room and saw her. At that moment, I lost all faith in the wonder drug. I sat at her bedside, leaned over, and prayed. Tears squeezed through my clenched eyes and splattered in a puddle on the floor. This woman was clearly dying. It doesn't take any prior experience to know what that looks like. We stayed at her bedside every day for four or five days, coming home only to sleep.

One night at about ten o'clock, Katie, Donpa and I stood in the hall outside her room and spoke in the familiar quiet murmurings behind closed doors. We were talking about what time we would come in the next day when Katie said, "She could die tonight." Her Dad nodded and said quietly, "Yes, she could." We hugged, then departed for home.

I fell into a deep sleep that night. In the midst of the stillness and deepness of my dark dreams, I suddenly felt a rush, a light, an energy across my chest. The pure, white energy shook through my body and woke me up. I sat up in bed, turned to Katie, and said, "She's gone."

Donpa called a few minutes later. The hospital had given him the news. We asked if he wanted us to come over, and he declined but said we would talk again in the morning.

Margaret died when she was fifty-four, and Katie was twenty-seven.

So, in the weeks before her mammogram, I understand when Katie walks me into grocery endcaps, ends sentences with "the," and turns out the bathroom light while I'm standing there brushing my teeth. She is justifiably distracted, overcome by raw terror.

I sit in the lobby at the hospital waiting for Katie to come out from her mammogram. From what she has described to me, this is not a pleasant procedure to undergo. Despite sitting in a waiting room furnished with nothing but worn out chairs and a stack of old magazines, I am, at the moment, the much more comfortable of the two of us.

I flip open a two-year-old copy of "R V Living." I read about water systems. I read the performance statistics on water pumps, tank capacity, filtration.

I read advertisements about generators: Amperage, decibels, fuel consumption rates, dry weights, dimensions.

I learn that a generator owner sees his generator on three occasions: When it is being installed, when it's being worked on, and when it's being replaced, so I suppose the color doesn't matter. They are a deep, muddy green. The kind of color one always gets when mixing any combination of mistake paints together. The manufacturer must get a good deal on mistake paint. Generators don't need to be good-looking, they need to be solid-looking, and have impressive performance statistics.

I flip from the generator ads to the generator article. I plunge into the article, "Recreational Vehicle Electric Generators: What To Look For, How to Buy."

Of course, I do not own a Recreational Vehicle and have no plans ever to do so. Accordingly, I do not own a Recreational Vehicle Electric Generator. I do not care about generators at all. I do not care about their performance statistics. I do not care about their amperage, decibels or size. Like their owners, I certainly do not care about their color.

But I am thankful for the subject because reading about Recreational Vehicle Electric Generators has brought me pure, continuous, blissful focus on a subject about which I do not care a whit. That which I care most about is in the next room with her chest in a vise, learning whether or not she has a tumor.

After twenty minutes, I now know all there is to know about generators, and stir briskly through the magazines to become expert on some other subject about which I do not care. Stirring through the magazine pile, I find a tattered two-year-old "Newsweek" magazine, with the then-latest week-old news. There is a private pilot magazine, the address tab with the prosperous doctor's name and address discretely torn off the corner.

My search abruptly ends as the door opens and Katie walks toward me. She looks at me for the first time in weeks, and she smiles. All clear.

*****

Shawn asks if he can ride his bike to the vacant lot around the corner. He wants to do some jumps from the vacant lot into the street. He assures me he can see the cars coming in time.

"No dice," I tell him.

So he promises to take his friend Ed along as flagman and observer. In other words, he promises to put his life in the hands of an eight-year-old.

"Well, maybe," I say.

Then he promises to put orange cones out on the street to alert oncoming drivers.

Fine. We have a deal. Katie and I leave Mikey in charge and go out for errands. On the way back, we notice that the cones are strewn and abandoned out on the street in front of the dirt lot. I prepare my lecture while we're pulling into the driveway, but Shawn walks over to the car, sticks his hand through the window and says, "Does this look broken to you?"

This stuff always happens on a weekend or a holiday.

We go into the house and begin first aid. I am so tired of first aid. We've done this way too many times.

"Shawn, do you still have that finger brace from your last broken finger?"

"No."

"How about the one from before?"

"They put a cast on it that time, Dad, remember?"

Barely. "Oh, yeah. Katie, do we have any Popsicle sticks?

"Like for crafts?"

"Yes."

"No."

"Okay, Shawn. Just try to hold your finger nice and still," I say.

"We have some Popsicles," my wife says.

"Good. Shawn, eat a Popsicle and I'll go look for some Scotch Tape."

"I don't like Popsicles."

"*I* do!" Vanessa gleefully intervenes. She rushes to the freezer and roots around for a Grape-Flavored Popsicle.

Shawn starts to complain that his finger is throbbing.

Michael stumps through the kitchen on his crutches, looking for food.

Shawn asks for an ice bag. Vanessa leans against the freezer, selflessly slurping on a Popsicle.

She turns, opens the freezer and looks for a bag of peas to use as an ice bag for Shawn. She only finds soybeans. Who ever eats soybeans? It's a good thing that we don't, or there would be nothing to put on Shawn's throbbing finger. Vanessa tugs on the bag to get it to come out of the wire rack in the freezer, but she can't get a good grip so she sets her Popsicle on the cutting board and then puts her entire tiny body behind the effort.

She gets the bag part way out, then it snags on the wire rack and splits wide open. Frozen soybeans fling everywhere and she flies back and lands on her behindus.

Michael stumps through the kitchen again, still searching for food. The rubber tip of his crutch smushes a soybean into a pancake with concentric circular ridges. Bull's-eye.

He opens the pantry and stares into its depths, oblivious to the nutritious frozen soybean buffet arrayed literally at his feet, then asks, *"Mom-what's-for-dinner?"*

Alex wanders into the kitchen and asks, innocently, "Mom, will you take me to the beach?"

"Which beach do you want to go to?" Katie asks.

"You've gotta be kidding," I interrupt.

Alex looks offended. "No fair. I haven't been to the beach for almost *three days*."

Poor thing.

"Alex," I state flatly, "There are other things going on right now."

I instruct Vanessa to get the dustpan out of the closet. She gets the dustpan in slow motion, spreads the soybeans, knocking a few under the fridge, which results in successfully bumping the project back on to me, with my one good arm.

Ahh, chasing down little green shriveled wads on the kitchen floor, how nice. They quickly soften and begin to turn into shiny obloid mushballs. A special moment.

Then I remember that the Popsicle is still on the cutting board and I rescue it just before it melts much, though it now has a (very small) Artificial Grape-Flavored Popsicle stain on it. Hardly noticeable.

I assign Shawn to finish Vanessa's Popsicle. He forces it down. I go to look for Scotch Tape again. I can't remember what interrupted me before. When I return with the tape, he proffers a purple smile and the newly barren Popsicle stick. I Scotch Tape his finger to the stick. Ah, the Wonders of Modern Medicine.

I have a poor track record with false negative fracture diagnoses. For example, last month with Mikey's broken foot. Or when Shawn broke his fingers (not this time, and not the prior time, but the time before that), I also missed the signs and he went for almost a week without care.

So this time, we're going to take Shawn to the Emergency Room just in case.

But I just have to say that, starting about three or four Emergency Room visits ago, something began to unravel inside me. I just can't make myself take him to the Emergency Room this time. It isn't that I get queasy. It's that I am just so completely burned out on going to the Emergency Room.

So, I send my wonderful wife. She takes my car because hers is in the shop. She leaves at noon.

Well, two o'clock comes but it's no problem. Then it's three. Four o'clock comes and I'm starting to get uptight, because eleven people are coming for dinner at 6:30, and I haven't been able to get to the store because we only have the one car. When she pulls into the driveway at 5:45, I frantically commandeer the car to rush off to the store to do some one-armed grocery shopping. As I speed away, window down, I hear her voice fading as she calls after me. She's saying, "Good news: It wasn't broken…"

✳✳✳✳✳

After two years, I just now heard from Robert. We were best friends in Junior High. He was my Best Man.

Rob has faded in and out of my life over the years, coming into and out of focus, sometimes sharp as a laser, other times diffuse and difficult to pin down.

He shows flashes of incredible genius, humor, insight, and then his personality or his person disappears. He's a comet that races into view, shines brightly, then skedaddles off to who-knows-where, for who-knows-how-long. I always try to encourage the marvel that is Robert, when Comet Robert is reflecting the brilliance of the sun.

Robert visited me during the time after I became a Christian, and before the day Katie and I were married.

Robert is a most engaging conversationalist and we talked for hours, about just about everything. He has a keen interest and insight on everything about life.

He asked why I had quit walking across the United States, why I had left USA Expedition.

Oh, boy. "Well," I said, "I think it was because, when I became a Christian, I could see that I was only glorifying myself, but I think God wanted me to glorify Him, instead." Gulp.

He asked what Christianity was all about, and I explained my beliefs and understanding as well I could, relying on what I'd learned up to that point.

We talked for most of an hour when suddenly, Robert said, "I want that. That's what's missing. I want to become a Christian."

So, we knelt, and prayed, right then and there on the living room floor.

And something flushed over him, some new kind of energy.

I had seen things flush over Robert before, but this time, it was as much from without as from within. That glow, the glow that is inside Robert, seemed to come out and reach for God, and a glow from God seemed to go into him, and I was there. And I thanked God for putting me there, and I could see that Robert was changed at that moment. No. It was more like Robert was *completed*, not changed. That energy he has had found its home.

I think God has him still, because God's love does not let go.

And at that moment, I blurted out, "Will you be my Best Man?" He agreed enthusiastically.

So, a few months later, when Katie and I got married, Rob was the Best Man. Then, two years ago this June, when Rob finally got married, he asked me to be *his* Best Man … well, sort of. He asked me to be the Co-Best Man.

The wedding was a few hundred miles away, and out in the country, so I flew up and rented a car. The night before the wedding Rob, Kalmia — his bride to be — several of their friends and I spent the evening in the big kitchen at the Community Arts Center drinking wine, improvising a gourmet dinner, and oh, yes, baking the wedding cake, did I mention?

As the evening wore on, I must have made five high-speed trips to the store for additional ingredients, me being the only one: a) in a condition to drive, and b) seemingly concerned about getting the cake done before, oh, say, the wedding. Robert had this "fabulous" recipe for a wedding cake.

By midnight we had concocted a mounded heap of flour, sugar, pineapple, cream cheese, heavy cream, assorted liqueurs and I forget what else but I do remember ending up out in the playground on one of those things that go round and round, looking up at spinning stars and feeling, actually, pretty good. We put the cake into the freezer and hoped it would "set up" and eventually stop oozing across the platter.

Kalmia still had to do payroll that night, and I heard later that she got home at about 2:00 a.m.

The next day (well, *that* day, for Kalmia) the wedding was held on a bridge in the country over a creek with the guests all seated on chairs in the adjoining meadow. A little artsy for me, but it's not my wedding. So far, so good.

So far, so good, that is, except the nearest place to park was about two miles away over dirt roads, and I pitched in and helped shuttle guests from the parking area to the meadow, again at about a hundred miles an hour, did I mention there were no seats in the van?

189

Did you know that if you go really, really fast over a washboard road, the vehicle begins to sort of float up off the surface and the ride becomes really, really smooth?

We're floating smoothly along as death whizzes past outside, but the wedding guests are oblivious because they are sitting on the metal floor of the van and they can't see out. Besides, I'm in formal clothes so I must know what I'm doing.

We careen around a corner and somebody asks, "What do we hang on to?" and someone else says, "We only have each other to hang on to," and then a third person says, dryly, "That's how Life is," and they chuckle, philosophers one and all.

According to the invitations, the wedding is at 12:00 noon.

Rippin' down the road at 12:06 p.m. with only three loads left to go, one of the ladies, in a flowery dress and wearing a big bonnet, skittering around on her behindus on the corrugated metal floor of the van says, "Well. I certainly *hope* they don't start the *wedding* without us. It would be *such* a *shame*. You know..." and with this, she turns to address her fellow sardines, "it's about *time* Robert *finally* got *married*! I'd *hate* to miss *this*!"

"Ma'am," I turned and said, "I'm the Best Man. You're not going to miss it."

190

Well that was a bit of a stretcher, not the part about not missing it, but the part about being the Best Man, because remember, I was the "Co-Best Man," well not exactly because the other "Co-Best Man" wasn't really a Man after all, but she was very nice, Rob's longtime dear friend Cynthia.

So Cynthia and I, a wonderful gal, were the "Co-Best Persons" as we stood on the bridge over the creek near the meadow in the country and it was all, well, so beautiful sure but more than anything, it was Artsy.

Artsy, Artsy, Artsy:

Tuxedos with Mandarin Collars for the wedding party. Well, not exactly Mandarin Collars because they didn't quite lay just right, so at the last minute we improvised by "releasing them to do their own thing." At this, they sproinged up and made a heck of a Nehru collar.

Well, not really a "heck of a" Nehru collar, but a "passable" Nehru collar which is fine because the guests really couldn't see us up on the bridge. They had to move the chairs way, *way* back that morning after discovering that they sunk into the mud when they were set up too close to the bridge.

We wore rented Plastic Tuxedo Shoes. (An anomaly, don't you think?)

There was a harpist, of course.

They wrote their own vows, well, not exactly "wrote," because Rob was still trying to think up some vows when the ceremony started, so he improvised by spluttering a few words, then retreating into tears to buy time until he thought of something more to say. He concluded mid-sentence with a loud, tearful, indistinct flourish, which was met with warm and empathetic applause from the guests, who were pretty much out of hearing range anyway.

It was officiated by a Minister of Sorts, or a Priestess, or some such being, Specially Bestowing Positive Vibrations of the Great Cosmic ... Whatever ... on the bride and groom.

Well, they said, "I Do" or, "I shall attempt to, to the extent it does not oppress me," or Whatever.

The wedding presents were things like:

A sundial.

Artsy stuff made out of burlap and twine and rusted iron that probably cost a whole lot more than you'd ever expect.

Batik ... printed ... fabric ... cloth ... things. I don't get what to do with big batik printed fabric cloth ... things. Apparently, they can be hung in the house as some sort of decor, or, by folding them, one can wear them a hundred different ways: scarves, dresses, scarves, sashes (what's a sash?) scarves again, things to put on one's head. In my world, I never see anyone wear them any way at all. But I do know that the only correct reaction is to say, "Ooh, it's so *beautiful!*" regardless of the pattern or colors or what the heck one does with it.

I had to catch my plane, and with wonderful, artsy feelings all around, I jumped into the car and rushed off.

Flying home, I thought, "As wonderful and fun as it all was, Something's Missing Here…"

I called Robert after a few months into his marriage, but the number wasn't working. I couldn't find a listing anywhere. The Post Office returned my letters. Two years passed.

So the other day, I got on the Internet and found an e-mail address for Robert.

Well.

He e-mailed me back to say that he and Kalmia were getting a divorce. Apparently he had some … inclinations … that he had not previously acknowledged to himself or others. She's leaving for Europe soon, and he's moving to San Francisco…

Robert accepted Christ, Robert became a Christian. I was there. Do his subsequent gods, distractions and detours in life invalidate his standing with his Savior? I don't think so. I hope not, because then I'd have to ask, do *mine?* Do *my* subsequent gods, distractions, and detours in life invalidate my standing with my Savior? So, I think

Robert is a Christian, and though he skims the earth like a comet, or wanders the streets of San Francisco looking for his next ... encounter, I think God has him still. And ever will. Not because Robert is deserving, but because God loves so deeply that He will not *abandon us* because we are sinners. Instead, He will *save us* because we are sinners. Of whom, I am the worst.

✳✳✳✳✳

It's Friday and I am standing out on the driveway by the cashier's table, holding the glass eyeball I have taken from the display case.

It looks so real. It even has fake blood-vessels. "Well, he *was* a Doctor," I tell myself, "so I suppose that is why he had this thing. It's such an accurate model, except that it's concaved—rather than round—in the back." There is a tiny sticker on it that says, "$5." I had noticed an assemblage of other old medical artifacts inside the house. You never know what you'll find at an estate sale.

As I am holding it, the cashier tells me that the Doctor had only one eye. The realization creeps over me that this was his eyeball, and I quickly hand it back to her.

Katie arrives a short time later. I feel an admittedly macabre urge to show her around the old house. The collected kitsch of a lifetime is displayed, stacked and heaped in the small rooms. The doctor's friends and relatives have already taken first dibs. Some of the rooms are off limits. Now neighbors and strangers are having at the carcass of the house, like the turkey after Thanksgiving, picked down to the bone by busy fingers, more eager than hungry.

We walk into the kitchen. Unopened bottles of prune juice, twenty cents. Great ocean view. The original kitchen cabinets. They'll probably tear them out. A 1970s era harvest gold refrigerator. Not For Sale. A silver ladle, which my wife buys. An old scalpel.

Katie has always wanted a fondue pot for sharing Christmas dinner with the family. We find a perfectly serviceable one — four bucks — but we somehow can't bring ourselves to buy it.

A vintage Italian ceramic egg basket with little chickys popping out the top, 2 bucks. We nab it.

I find some irresistible 50's era Hawaiiana Kitsch: A genuine combination ashtray/pipe holder with a volcano in the middle of it, inscribed, "MADE IN HAWAII WITH LAVA BY COCO JOE." Four bucks, and I don't own a pipe. I nab it. A Tiki-mask bottle-stopper that says HAWAII on the back. I nab it, too. They probably sell for two bucks in Hawaii. I pay four.

My favorite thing, the "find" of the whole sale, is a shot glass, well not really a shot glass. I found it with some other medical artifacts. It's a big three-ounce glass and it's shaped like a shot glass, but on the front, it says:

PHOSPHO-SODA

(FLEET)

For active elimination

On the back are tablespoon and ounce gradient lines and the instructions, "Follow with full tumbler of water." The perfect oversized shot glass for that special guest.

And an odd thing: a pen holder/thermometer—a paperweight, really—with little strike marks all around the tiny little hole that the pen goes into. He had missed the hole a lot—after all, he only had one eye. Why not use a pen cup? Did he like the little challenge of trying to put the pen in the holder? He wasn't a very good shot.

Over the days, neighbors and strangers, like ants (or aunts) render the place down to the bone.

It's Saturday and I return, drawn again to the old house. Though I'd had fun buying kitsch the prior day, now I'm being pulled back here more from a sense of duty, than desire.

When you live into your nineties, after a long, full life, having accumulated learning and accomplishments, a grain or a pebble or a truckload at a time, having piled it

196

up, put it out there, said, "Here's all of my stuff. Here I am," it isn't fair to foul out of the ballgame and into obscurity on a technicality (that technicality being death). Somebody, somewhere, ought to be able to hold you up and say, at the very least, "Here is who he was." That is what I am doing now.

Dr. Michael A. Macallan, "Dr. Mac," Navy doctor, longtime resident, lived into his nineties, practiced for more than fifty years, married twice, blinded in one eye, neighbor, never met him, didn't know him.

But I know this, Doctor: You lived, you died, and afterwards, you made it into this book.

A man is standing at the cashier's table. He is wearing Lee jeans, a handmade leather belt, a cowboy hat with a custom braided leather band. His watch band is one of those solid silver bracelets with bits of turquoise set into it. He is thin and gangly, with dark stringy hair. He is fortyish (Or twentyish? Maybe fiftyish? "Weather and ciggys and drink all conspire, to make Father Time out to seem like a liar.") Custom eel skin cowboy boots. He looks like the kind of guy I've seen working his table at every Arts and Crafts Fair I've ever been to.

Then I notice, staring up from his finger, Dr. Mac's glass eyeball. He is fiddling with it, trying to decide whether to buy it and make a ring out of it. A dead man's glass eyeball estate sale ring.

He slowly, deliberately places the eyeball on each successive finger, leans back, cocks his head, stretches out his arm, extends his fingers, and takes in the effect. I think to myself, "It's a goner," but suddenly, he straightens and quickly hands it back to the cashier, a bit repulsed. I didn't think guys like that could be repulsed. I sigh with relief.

I don't know who you are, heirs of Dr. Macallan, and maybe I need to take the log out of my own eyeball before I talk about the splinter in yours, but I think you don't sell your dead ancestor's glass eyeball at his estate sale for five dollars, minus thirty percent to the people running the sale, divided up by twenty or so heirs, and everybody ends up with seventeen and a half cents. I mean, who gets the odd penny?

Can I quickly just tell you what you do? Ahem: Throw it into the coffin before they snap it shut and even if it's a spare glass eyeball not his favorite glass eyeball you let it go into the grave with some modicum of dignity for heaven's sake, O.K. ? Can we drop it now?

I go into the house. Yep, they're still there: The house is still filled with every single academic degree that he ever earned. High School. College. Med School. Internship. Specialized training. Awards of Merit. They date over seventy years.

A man's whole life. All his accomplishments. A buck a piece, two bucks for the ones in the nicer frames.

That's not for me to buy. The heirs should take those, stack them in a box and stick 'em in an attic, please.

There is a picture frame and in it, a photo of Dr. Mac at his retirement party, decades prior. Friends and co-workers with tight smiles stand about ten or twelve feet back from him. He is alone, standing with his own tight smile. Enclosed in the frame along with the photo is a retirement card which all of his friends have signed.

Two bucks. Who's gonna buy something like that at an estate sale?

Finally, I have to ask the people running the sale, "Didn't he have any heirs?" They tell me that he did, and that they've already taken all the mementos that mattered and that they wanted and besides they're getting up in years themselves, and there was a divorce, and the first wife is dead, and the second wife is dead, and there are no kids from the second marriage, and the kids from the first wife are now in their seventies, and maybe not real keen on their Dad having divorced their mother and remarried. The divorce was decades ago and the parties are dead, yet it continues to tear at the fabric of this family.

It's Sunday so everything's half price. I return on a final salvage mission. By now, most of the stuff is gone. We're getting down to the bones. The lady running the sale asks me if I live in the neighborhood because she wants to know how many trash bags the garbage men will pick up at a time.

The eyeball has been sold. When I ask about it, the cashier says a friend of hers bought it to put it up for auction on eBay.

I salvage old photos, taken six or seven decades ago. Some show frumpy old relatives sitting in the parlor in dark, ancient — even then — clothes and ridiculous hats.

Other pictures show vibrant young friends canoeing on the lake, playing badminton, posing at poolside, shooting archery, riding horseback, out on picnics. There's a picture of the brother who became a priest — there's always a brother who became a priest. There are people on the promenade deck of a passenger ship. Coming over? Going to? They have the look of the Olde World.

There is a picture of the former future Dr. Mac himself, leaning back in an armchair, smiling, confident, Wellington boots propped up, wool suit, vest, Ascot tie, gold watch chain, pipe clenched in teeth, dapper, twenty-something.

A picture of a young woman, (wife number one?) eager, hopeful. A picture of a child on a tricycle. The woman again a few years later, still young, in a wheelchair, still eager, willing, lonely, sad. The woman, sitting on the living room floor, wheelchair out of picture, skirts covering legs, in front of the fireplace, the hearth immaculate, a well-kept home. Homely, eager to please, lost. The woman again, older still, hopeful, abandoned, lonely, sad, puzzled. Like a once-fine dog, life gone by, somehow knowing there will soon come a new puppy.

I buy a Parker Fountain and Ballpoint Pen Set on a marble stand with a brass plate that says, "DR. MAC." I bet it was his retirement gift. It has never been used.

I buy—salvage, really—the plaque from his office door. "DR. MACALLAN." It's made out of white marble with square black letters etched into it. It looks like something from an old black and white movie. (There were always scenes in offices in old black and white movies.) But none of his heirs will ever say, "Look honey, here is the plaque your great great granddaddy had on his office door years ago. Did you know he was a doctor in the war? And look, his degrees. Here's a picture of his grandparents..."

At the cashier's table they tell me that this tiny old house sold in less than an hour, for more than asking price. The new owners plan to tear it down and build a bigger one.

On Monday, a tidy row of black trash bags lines the curb. The garbage truck comes along, they throw the bags into the crusher and drive off. It is finished. The dismantling of a lifetime. The parceling out. The rendering down, no matter what we do, that's how it ends up, whether after ninety years or ninety days.

I behave myself for a week or two, but then I can't help it: I look on eBay. There, in living color, I find Dr. Mac's Irish Blue Eyeball. The bid is up to fifteen bucks.

Strange that no matter how much sand a man uses to build his castle, the evening tide, death, washes it all away. By morning, it's back to smooth beach. I guess there needs to be room for the next castle.

This morning I opened the boxful of kitsch I had bought and spread out his belongings on my table. I picked out the unused retirement gift pen set, and gave the pen a click. "Okay, Dr. Mac," I said, "It's time. Let's tell your story … "

JULY

It's July and the sprinkler system is finished: Katie will never again have to stand out in the yard with her thumb over the end of the hose.

I am out in the yard, barefoot and content, with a bag of seed, a spreader, a roller, and twenty five hundred pounds of topper. I've killed off all the old "lawn" over the course of the month with several treatments of herbicide.

The sun bakes into my body. As I sweat underneath my coveralls, I am happy. It's good to be barefoot in the yard on a hot July day. I am being filled up by life. Over the last few months, slowly, I have reversed the flow of life energy: I'm no longer filling life, life is filling me. Every detail of nature, of life, that I take in, compounds my sense of delight, my appreciation for being alive.

My shoulder feels better. Mikey is out of his cast. Everyone's healthy. Life is good.

I am refreshed.

I am going to take my refreshed self and family and get out of town for several weeks. It is a luxury to have the time to take a vacation when you don't "need" a vacation. I am already in a full time vacation mode. I get to take my relaxed and refreshed self on an adventure.

After that, let life throw at us what it will: Life is still good. My sense of joy and well-being seems to have returned and become a permanent part of my outlook, after eluding me for decades.

After our family trip, I plan to tear into the challenges and joys of building a new future, perhaps a new career. Bring it on.

The sun is setting as I finish spreading the last few bags of topper over our newly seeded lawn. It's one of those embracing summer nights that says, "Hello, here is a new opening in time for you. Enjoy the ancient feelings of a warm summer night."

In the fall, my shoulders urge me to scurry inside when the sun sets, but not tonight. Tonight as the sun sets, the world outside opens up and welcomes me into a new "day," filled with its own possibilities, its own identity. It is an embracing, more comfortable version of a summer day, filled with energy, hope, and possibility.

So often during the year when the sun sets, I feel a small inner remorse that the day is done and gone. Not so with certain July nights. In July, there are nights like tonight when the sun takes its leave and the world wakes up. The temperature drops and the fresh evening air embraces my whole body. Ah, summer nights!

It's late by the time I finish enjoying the sunset and the transition to night. I take a shower and change out of my coveralls, and then Katie and I are on our way to Santa Barbara.

Katie and I are going on a second honeymoon. My Bikey is racked onto the back of our Suburban. With its fat tires, two sets of foot pegs and a milk crate zip tied onto the back fender, my Bikey can take us on adventures anywhere, and return with a few souvenirs in the crate to boot.

We arrive late in Santa Barbara and I look for an over-sized parking space while Katie gets the room key. We can see the ocean from our balcony when we stand in just the right spot.

The next morning, we unload the bike and go off on a tour. On the way to the adjacent community of Montecito we take a side trip through the cemetery. The setting is lovely, near the ocean, the landscaping is lush and there are little roads all through the grounds. We stop at the far end of the cemetery, look out over the ocean, and hold each other.

When it's time to leave, it's a little difficult to find our way out again because of the narrow little roadways which lace the grounds like a maze. They all look alike, and none of them is really going anywhere.

A story pops into my head for a *Twilight Zone* sort of episode: Two people drive through a cemetery. At the far end, they stop and look out over the ocean. They hold each other. Something happens, they each experience some sort of break or interruption or flash in the continuity of their consciousness. They don't mention this to each other because everything still seems fine afterward.

But when they try to leave, they can't seem to find the exit. Hours go by, yet the sun doesn't move. Birds sing, trees rustle in the breeze. It's a beautiful day that seems to go on and on forever.

Trapped, they pass the same tombstones over and over and after a while, decide to make a game of reading them and eventually, they know their way around the cemetery, having read every tombstone.

Later, they notice that a funeral service is finishing up at the other end of the cemetery. They drive over and arrive just as the grave workers are putting the last of the dirt on the graves and setting the tombstones into place. They approach the graves, curious to read the new tombstones, and find that their own names are on them. Cue the discordant music, the disturbing camera angles, the Rod Serling speech:

"What happened to these two young lovers in their final moments? What took them into another dimension as they stood at the edge of a cemetery and looked out over the frontier of the ocean? What did they encounter there in that place between the infinite and the finite, that place and time which we know as ... The Twilight Zone."

Cue the star field, The End, roll the credits.

We find the exit (of course) and meander down a one-way road which we discover empties out at the Biltmore Hotel on the beach. As we ride about town throughout the morning our approach is, whenever we find an interesting looking road, we turn onto it. If we see a place we like, we stop to experience it.

By midday we are in Montecito. The aroma of garlic pulls us into the Palazzio Trattoria Italiana. Wine is self-served from a tap, and we track the number of glasses with a crayon on the paper tablecloth.

After lunch, we find a small road that turns into a smaller road that turns into a trail. We cut through on the trail and it brings us out at another road at the base of the mountains. We park near a creek and hike up the trail next to it.

We find a place where the creek flattens out into a wide, clear, shallow pool, then cuts into a rockslide and spills into a deep, round pool. We spend the day splashing and playing and sliding into the pool. The sun bakes the boulders and they radiate their heat long into the afternoon. They feel warm and inviting and, somehow even soft when we drape ourselves over them between swims, drying out, basking in nature's makeshift armchairs. This is a day that should never end.

Late in the afternoon we head downhill toward town on yet another new road. We pass a house I've seen in my dreams. I stop and turn us around to head up the hill, back to the house. I stop. Yup. This is it. This is the direction I always see the house from in the dream. There is the promontory where the road curves near the concrete front steps, a little too close to the road. There's the dark brown wooden siding. Huge trees. A nice bit of property —not too much, but large enough for a man to move around on. There's the outbuilding, a fixed-up barn and sure enough, there's the glow of the neon sign peeking out through the partly opened sliding barn door. The weather's warm and sunny today, but in the dream I am on the road, traveling, and it's cold and getting dark and starting to rain when I discover this place.

A neon sign is the universal symbol of welcome to the wayfaring road warrior I once was. Neon means, "You can come in here." In my dream, and here before me, this place is not a little roadhouse, but a home, my home, sort of. My retreat, my place where I come to connect with those people and endeavors most important to me, and to disconnect from all that doesn't really matter. In my dream, I buy it because it turns out to be a place that to my surprise really exists. The property isn't for sale, so I have to pay more than it's worth to buy it, but somehow I afford it and the sting of overpaying quickly wears off and I never regret buying it because people—important people, good people, vibrant, intelligent, purposeful, significant, connected and involved people come here and their ideas flow without limit and turn into dreams and even become realities, bigger and better than the way they first dreamed it. The property is large enough and simple enough to incubate the biggest of ideas into realities.

I shut off the bike. "Katie, I saw this place in my dreams. I'm gonna buy it some day."

"Okay."

I start up the bike and we roll back into town. We have wine and cheese on the balcony of our room, a peek at the ocean, and a perfect day comes to an end.

Our last day in Santa Barbara. We take the motorcycle to Hope Ranch and ride around on the "country" roads. Well, not really "country," because this is one of the most exclusive neighborhoods in the world. Yet I am a sucker for winding roads on my motorcycle, regardless of median household incomes. We spend the morning covering the Ranch and getting lost (whatever that means) as much, and as often as possible.

We have lunch at Left Turn At Albuquerque in downtown Santa Barbara. Though the food, service and margaritas are terrific, the best thing about "Left Turn" is the ambiance. Not the ambiance in the place, but the ambiance adjacent to it. Large sliding doors open up the front of the building and tables spill onto the patio with no real defining line between indoors and out. Out on the sidewalk, the panoply moving past represents every known life form. This is true Santa Barbara. The sun has a special quality here which makes everyone, even the local characters, look good and important and purposeful and healthy. In Santa Barbara, everybody looks like somebody who is good friends with somebody who is really, really famous.

After what may have been one too many gourmet Margaritas, we go to the downtown mall. I find a little outdoor cart that sells hats and on impulse I pop one on Katie's head. She's cute.

There is always a little inner monologue to justify any purchase. My monologue to justify the hat is rather odd. I've never bought her a hat. She never wears hats. The monologue goes like this: "I've never seen her in a hat. She looks cute in a hat. I wonder why she never wears hats. Maybe because her Grandma and her mother had to wear hats when they got cancer. Well, if she ever has to wear a hat, she'll be cute. She's cute in it now. I'll buy it now."

In Macy's she buys a pair of cute tennis shoes and some little anklet socks. With her new hat, shoes, and socks, she is absolutely adorable, beaming, and giggly. It's nice to see her feel good about shopping. Katie is a born shopper, and I have neglected all these years to tell her how much I appreciate her going out and bringing back to our home all of those things which help to make our lives lovely.

On the way out of town, we stop to take an hours-long walk on the beach. The tide is low and the warmth hugs our every move, and I feel like I can walk along the beach forever, endlessly curious about what might be revealed in the next cove. We don't return to the car until just before sunset. We drive up to Cambria.

Katie has selected a quaint and quiet Bed & Breakfast surrounded by lovely large trees and meandering gardens. The office is closed by the time we arrive, but there is a note on the door instructing us where to find the key to get into our room.

The cute little room is wonderfully "B & B," with a large stone fireplace, one of those beds that's about three feet off the ground, and a chest filled with quilts at the foot of the bed. Frankly, it's a little more "cutesy" than I would want for my home, (one too many cross-stitched framed quotes on the wall) but it's just right for a B & B room.

I get up to use the restroom in the middle of the night. When I turn out the light to come back to bed, I cannot, of course, see a thing. Katie, on the other hand, can see me perfectly because her eyes are still adjusted to the darkness. I amble from the bathroom with my arms waving out in front of me, a gait not entirely unlike Frankenstein's.

Katie and I are in the habit of amusing ourselves by watching one another wander about when the other's eyes haven't adjusted. Tonight, I put on quite a show. On the way back from the bathroom, I clunk into the chest at the foot of the bed and sprawl forward, disappearing in a flash below the horizon of the mattress, splattering myself on the chest, then bouncing up, off, and crashing onto the floor with a giant THUD, my skull barely missing the stone hearth. It seems like it takes a long time to finally hit the floor — probably all those stops on the way down. Fortunately for her, I make enough noise that she can pretend I woke her up.

"Are you okay, Johnny?"

"I thust thlipped on the chetht," I slur into the carpet, where I am planted face first. "I'm not thure."

"Oh, Honey…" she offers sympathetically.

I climb back into bed. "Ow. I think I'm okay, but I just hurt all over."

She reaches over and gently hugs me. "Sorry," she says. "Do you need me to do anything?"

"No."

We lay there in silence for a moment. I hear a muffled little snicker. Then another, finally she just lets it out, giggling uncontrollably.

The image of her beloved, descending inexorably below the horizon, helpless and blind, was just too hilarious not to savor. Once she knows I don't need an ambulance, she re-enacts my sightless fall in her mind: Here's Dufus, groping about, smacking the chest with toe, disappearing helplessly below the horizon of the foot of the bed. The thuds, the grunts, each movement of the slow motion ballet a delight to recall. She laughs off and on for a good ten minutes, yawns, rolls over, and falls back to sleep.

The prettiest, longest, warmest, sunniest day ever:

The next morning we take the bike off the rack and head out for a ride into the countryside to discover the "Lost Wineries" of Paso Robles.

Santa Rosa Creek Road takes us out of town, past houses and farmland, the floor of the valley filled with huge trees, which long ago tapped into groundwater alongside the creek. This is the "old road" to Paso Robles, the one used before highway 46 was built. The large homes diminish as we get further away from Cambria and climb into wilder country. We turn onto Mountain Drive, a dirt road, which takes us up to the "back of the back of the backcountry." There we find old mines and mining camps. I have always loved exploring isolated backcountry roads, and the bike with its big fat tires is perfect for this.

We discover the Carmody McNight winery, which isn't even on our map of "Lost Wineries." Gary Carmody and his wife, Marian McNight, have developed a lovely spot buried deep in the backcountry of the Lost Wineries. Gary is a retired television and film actor and his wife is a former Miss America. Katie and I taste wine samples from the quaint little tasting room, then order glasses of our favorite and sit out on Adirondack chairs under immense oaks. Our spot overlooks the vineyards and the pond and the guesthouse, which is surrounded by a swim-to-the-doorstep pool. The only sound is that of the oak trees whispering "thank you" to the breeze while Andrea Boccelli serenades us through speakers somewhere up in the branches.

We sip our wine and eat the best bread I've ever tasted from their family Beer Batter Bread Recipe. Not too bad.

Twenty years of layering, twenty years of work, twenty years of winding the mainspring ever tighter have come to a halt, and now the mainspring is unwinding. I feel younger each day. I no longer wear a wristwatch, but if I did, I'm certain that at this moment, it would be slowly ticking backwards.

I have not got a care in the world. We have enough money, enough time, good health and each other. I am enjoying the world that God has given us, close up. I could not be more content.

After acquiring a few bottles of our favorite vintages and securing them in the milk crate, we are on our way. We had planned to visit several other wineries, but after Carmody McNight, we have an "it can't get any better than this" contentment.

It can, however, get *cooler* than this, and we head to Lake San Antonio for a dip. Along the way, Katie and I ride as one. When I lean the bike into a long, gorgeous curve, she leans with me, trusting me, trusting the bike. I don't know if the road between Carmody McNight and Lake San Antonio is the most beautiful road in the world — it is certainly quite beautiful, with long, wide, steep curves, no traffic, rollicking hills, which dip us down into bountiful valleys dotted with little farm houses — but when we ride it, the two of us trust the bike and the road and each other, and that is what makes this the most beautiful road in the world.

It is at least a hundred and five degrees at Lake San Antonio, and we ride along the lakefront road until we discover a quiet little cove for ourselves. There is no parking nearby but because we are on the motorcycle, we are able to squeeze it safely to one side of the road. We peel down to our swimsuits and jump in. The lake bottom is squishy between our toes with the kind of soggy mud that man-made lakes always seem to have. The water is chilly and refreshing and quickly contrasts with the too-hot day. A surprisingly short time later, we're too cold and we wade to shore, where we are instantly baked dry. We spend the afternoon happily ping-ponging between too hot and too cold.

After we get our riding gear back on and get on the bike, we ride perhaps a mile before we are just too darn hot again. We park at the public beach and swim out to the large floating platform tethered off shore.

Midday has lasted forever. We pull ourselves onto the platform and again are instantly dried. We sit, soaking in the sun.

Katie starts to giggle.

"It *is* nice, isn't it?" I say, mistaking her mirth for simple *joie de vivre.*

This makes her giggle more. Then she laughs uncontrollably. She pulls it together, rubbing her eyes. Then she looks over at me, just sitting there on the platform being a nice man, and busts out laughing again.

"What?"

It takes her some time to control herself. Finally she is able to push out, "You. Last night." She loses it again. I think, "Any romantic mishaps last night?" Then I realize she is re-living my sightless tumble over the chest at the end of the bed. She's re-hearing the thunk, replaying my blank-eyed grappling with the air, re-observing the Newtonian arc of my helpless fall, followed once again by the inimitable crashing and groaning.

After five minutes of unquenchable mirth on her part, I'm plenty warm and ready to swim back, but she is still finishing up. Finally, she composes herself and suggests we swim back. Good idea.

She says, "I'll get in first, and you follow me to make sure I'm okay. But don't follow too close. I don't like to be bothered when I swim."

She jumps off the side and heads toward shore. I stand there for a moment, baking, letting her get a little way ahead.

The water is deep. She is not a very strong swimmer. I jump in and swim after her. I time it perfectly, reaching her midway between the platform and the shore. I grab her by the ribs and tickle her relentlessly. She panics and swallows water and thumps me on top of the head over and over with her fist, whining that it isn't funny. My turn to giggle uncontrollably, until the fingernails come out: she means business so I swim away. I reach shore first and turn around. She can touch the bottom now, but she spends a few minutes fluttering about in the shallows, probably trying to erase the memory of her being tormented. Maybe the memory of my nocturnal nose dive will be erased along with it.

By the time she emerges from the water, she has moved past it, which is good because I appreciate the James Bond 007/Ursula Andress-ness of the moment much more than I would if she were still mad. Katie is a perfectly beautiful creature. Yikes!

I hand her a towel. She says, "You're bleeding." I look at my shoulder. It's bleeding from her fingernails. She apologizes. Sort of. Actually, she says three things: 1) she doesn't forgive me for tickling her, and 2) she doesn't apologize for me forcing her to defend herself, but 3) she's sorry that I'm bleeding. She really is. She hides a smile.

I love her.

After two big cold bottles of iced tea and a map check, we depart for Cambria, backtracking through the wine country. Our shadow casts across the road. It is hard to distinguish in our silhouette where one of us ends and the other begins.

Just before sunset, at the top of the canyon road that will take us out of the mountains and down into Cambria, I stop to put on my riding gloves. Katie takes a stretch. Suddenly, she freezes and whispers, "Look." At the summit of the hill next to the road, we see a small dome the color of dried grass, with points sticking up on each side. Below that are the vertical slits of two yellow eyes. Mountain lion. As we watch, he locks eyes with us and his head sinks slowly into the grass, disappearing completely. We now have no idea where he is, but we are certain we are still being watched. We jump on the bike and get out of there, leaving one glove behind.

The temperature plummets soon after the sun goes down. My ungloved hand is freezing so I decide to turn around and retrieve my glove. We return to the spot, but the glove is gone. There have been no cars passing in either direction. We fire up the bike and get out of there. Why would I tempt fate?

We shiver down the canyon and at last arrive in town. At our B&B, we sit our saddle sore selves on pillows on the hearth and enjoy some of that fine wine from Carmody McKnight. Pretty darn good day.

Inspired by Carmody McKnight's fine product, I compose An Poeym in Four Parts to the perfect day. This rhyming stuff, it isn't easy. This next one might sound really cheesy, so with apologies to everyone, everywhere, I present, with great hesitation:

JOHN VALDEZ

AN POEYM,
"ODE TO A PERFECT DAY"
By John Valdez

PART ONE: ODELETTE (#2) TO MY BIKEY

"It takes up space," she used to say,
"Your 'Bikey' just gets in the way."

"Kate, the space it takes, you know,
Is any place we want to go."

Today I proved my bike works fine
Conveying Kate and me and wine.

It's been redeemed, Kate likes it now.
(Although her tail-end still says, "Ow!")

'Cuz it can take us, just we three
To anywhere we want to be.

It's good on pavement, good on trails, you
find it cures whatever ails you.

We meld together, lean as one
The three of us have so much fun.

PART TWO: ODELETTE TO CARMODY McKNIGHT

To rhyme with Carmody McNight
Gives e'en seasoned poets fright.
I daren't try it … well, I might:

I'm glad that Gary Carmody
Left H'wood with its finery
To open his McWinery

When we got there, we were fed
The World's Best Beer Batter Bread.
(And wine that went straight to our head.)

Then, serenaded from the sky,
Bocelli nearly made us cry.

PART THREE: ODELETTE TO LAKE SAN ANTONIO, AND TO SWEET REVENGE

The lake was squishy on our feet.
Still, it helped us beat the heat.

And after last night's chest swan dive
I'm awful glad to be alive

I tumbled, hapless to the earth
This happ'ly filled my wife with mirth.

Dare snicker at my trials and tribs?
Then fingers — mine — will rake your ribs!

221

JOHN VALDEZ

PART FOUR: ODELETTE. THE CONCLUSION
OF THE MATTER

My neck, in back, has straight up hair:
My glove was on the road somewhere
Then dragged into a lion's lair.
I wouldn't want to wear it there.

When big cats vanish, but see me,
On Bikey's where I want to be.

It's pained and sálved our tail ends
Our Bikey is our bestest friend.

If I could pick, I'd have to say
That we just had the Greatest Day

Love, adventure, blisters, bliss
I couldn't ask for more than this.

(This rhyming stuff, it isn't easy.
Sorry if it sounded cheesy.)

In the morning we drive up the coastline. From Cambria to Ragged Point, the highway skims over hills and pastures that slope gently to the sea. The terrain changes at Ragged Point and the highway alternates between hugging the steep cliffs with raw, breathtaking views, then tucking back into the small creek valleys, bunched with forest. This is one of the most scenic and popular sections of the famous Highway One.

Years ago, while returning from a business trip to San Francisco, I spotted a remote cluster of large old buildings and trees from the airliner. They were nestled in a pastoral setting with nothing nearby for miles around—a secret Shangri-La. Later, I researched my find and determined that I had spotted Mission San Antonio De Padua, the "Lost Mission." I vowed to visit someday.

Like today. Though it means leaving the beauty of Highway One, Katie and I cut off the highway at Kirk Creek and climb Nacimiento Fergusson Road up and away from the coast. The puffs of fog fade behind us and we travel the road rarely taken through stands of oak, across creeks, over and around long rolling hills—my favorite type of countryside, the way I imagine Heaven to be. We travel this way for over twenty miles, never seeing another car or building. Finally we come to a nondescript intersection where a small sign points us toward the Mission.

JOHN VALDEZ

Mission San Antonio de Padua, founded in 1771 by Father Juan Junipero Serra, is one of twenty-one Catholic Missions established in California among the indigenous peoples. But unlike the missions at the sites of modern-day cities like Los Angeles, San Francisco, San Diego and San Jose, no city or town ever developed around this mission, and it remains remote today, just as in Serra's time. I love this stuff. I love finding the most remote places, where civilization took root, faltered, and reverted to wildness.

When we first get out of the car, the air is inert and so silent that we fight a panicky feeling to get right back in and leave. It is so very still and quiet and remote and unpopulated.

Our first impression—that nothing is happening, or has happened out here, *for* a long, long time—is superseded by a new impression, a sense that things have indeed happened here, *over* a long, long time. People have been born here, baptized here, lived here, married here, worked here, grown old and died and were buried here, and our bodies slowly sense the centuries-long accumulation of all of this, which is as it should be, for each of we individual humans descend, by the thread of our own true story, from some similarly primitive and ancient place, somewhere on this earth. It's good and proper that humans retain a sense

224

for knowing when we are in a place where ancestors carved out a way to live.

Wells and irrigation ditches were dug by hand and lined with stone, one at a time. Then used, then abandoned. Water and wind and time wore at them, unchallenged, and they slowly settled and filled and all that remains of that hard hot work under the sun, sweat of the brow, is the uneven rows of the tops of a few stones, poking up along the edges where there were once life-giving wells and ditches. We appreciate the long-ago work, because, in their day, the wells and the canals were the reason food could grow and people could survive, and have children, and work and live and die in this vast space in the heart of a beautiful countryside, mostly forgotten, today remembered, existent now, where the delicious air speaks through the silence. By the time we have to go, we are fighting an urge to stay long enough to absorb, in our beings, the gift and hard work of preparing a place to become a *place*. Leaving feels a bit disrespectful. We don't have to go. That is a construct, an acquired reflex, a default to artificial urgency that modernity prescribes, a reflex that this place of continuous "now" does not recognize or understand. But we are hopelessly steeped in the mindset of modern people, for whom an hour in such a place is an eternity. We go.

JOHN VALDEZ

We arrive late in Carmel, where Katie has rented a cozy little upstairs room at the Green Lantern Inn.

The room comes stocked with nighttime eye covers, a luxury I haven't previously experienced. For several years, I've worn earplugs when I sleep, and now with the additional discovery of eye covers I blissfully blank out all evidence that there is a reality. I sleep dreamlessly for about eleven hours.

During a mid-morning walk to the town park, a long-time local tells us about The Clint Eastwood "Ranch" on the outskirts of town. He tells us The Ranch has a bar where folks sit around the piano and sing old time ballads of simpler days gone by. For us, these are the simpler days, right here and now. Still, it sounds fun.

Midday, we ride the motorcycle down to Carmel River State Beach, one of the most beautiful spots in the world, where the Carmel River meets the sea in a sunny little cove. The seawater is clear and cool, the beach warm and wide. Pillows of fog bob along the cliffs down the coastline to the south of us, playing games with the quality of light under their shadows.

I swim in the cool, icy, delicious, tingly sea, indulging every sense. When I get out, the summer sun quickly dabs me dry and warms me deep inside, another delight.

An afternoon of shopping in town, dinner and a bottle or so of wine at Mondo's Trattoria, and we're off into the night to search for "The Ranch." After a few wrong turns, we eventually pull into the gravel parking lot. I instantly love this place: vast and rustic and real. We enter the bar through the back door, as the long-time local had suggested, and find a grand piano surrounded by an assortment of young and old, local and wayfarer, rich and poor, wistfully singing old tunes, just as he said we would.

At first it's a little awkward because we feel too shiny, new, young and happy to fit in, but after an Irish Coffee or two, our shoulders relax and we lean into the piano and we remember more songs than we remembered we remembered.

I sit next to the pianist. Next to me is Katie. Going around the piano, the next is a local fellow with once-yellow bib overalls, now splattered with the paint colors of a thousand projects, other people's projects. He has a rim of fine silver hair, and here and there around the perimeter of his baseball cap his shiny bald scalp peaks out. He requests arcane Irish ballads from the prior century and as he sings, hitting every note and every lyric, he stares sadly off into times and traumas unseen, as though he were himself the original subject of, or inspiration for, each song.

Next to him is a local lady in her fifties, stocky and overweight, wearing the kind of glasses where the bow dips down and connects to the bottom of the frame. Her hair is cut short along the sides and is longer and curly on

227

top. She goes for show tunes. She works for the school district and lives in one of the trailer parks tucked back in the canyons.

The father and son next to her, both wearing similar V-neck sweaters are cordial, smiley, friendly, happy, a little aloof. The Dad, late fifties, naturally knows a lot more of the songs than the thirtyish son, and in the banter between them, I learn that, after golfing Pebble Beach for several days, they are now stuck here due to mechanical troubles with their private jet, and are waiting for new parts to be flown in; hostages of—and marooned by—their own wealth. A pity.

But The Ranch knows no class or caste, and our singing is earnest if not sophisticated. Hours later, the place closes down and we all walk out, friends, arm-in-arm, tunelessly crooning snippets of newly learned ancient ditties, brothers and sisters, completely content.

We find our way back to our room at the Green Lantern Inn.

The next morning I awaken on top of the bedcovers, face down, still dressed, my feet hanging over the edge of the bed, shoes on, the room door wide open and the key still in the lock. Whew!

July is officially over and today we get to pick up our kids.

AUGUST

All four of our children are flying into San Jose. Katie and I cut our breakfast short and leave Carmel early in order to be at the airport well in advance of our children's arrival.

Parenting causes people to think in funny ways. On our way to the airport, we each think, and, at different times say out loud, that we wish we were ALL on that airplane. Translation: If the kid's plane crashes, we want to be with them so we could all die together.

Well, the plane arrives safely — of course — and our beautiful, bright sparkling children file off and into our arms. We hug them and kiss them and help carry their bags to the car, pay the parking ransom, and are out of there.

We travel up the east side of the bay, cross the San Rafael bridge and reconnect with Highway 101. We shoot through Petaluma and into Santa Rosa, where Katie has reserved a room.

The hotel is everything described in the book, plus a few things not described, such as having a back window right on the highway. Now, I'm not a snob so much as a light sleeper, and the instant I take a look at this place, I think, "Nope. I ain't stayin' there."

So we pull out the B&B guide and find a place in Healdsburg that has a guest house over the garage. The rate for two rooms and a kitchen is about 20% less than we were going to pay for one room on the highway, breakfast is included, and it is set in a vineyard. Sounds pretty good.

It *is* pretty good. About two miles outside of Healdsburg, at the Inn With No Name, we are shown to our rooms, on the second story over the garage, separate and beautifully decorated, with a lovely vineyard and forever views from the black-bottom pool.

This is the kind of place I wish I could spend more time in. We drive into town, have a sumptuous dinner on the square, and return, late, to our room. I doze off vaguely hoping our innkeeper is not another Norman Bates. No one on the planet knows we are here.

We wake up mid-morning and all go swimming in the black-bottom pool. The air is about 85 degrees, the pool about 70, the views endless. Afterward, we say our goodbyes and are on our way to Mendocino and the "Lost Coast."

In Mendocino, we stay at the Cabot Cove Inn, well, not really. One side of the sign says, "Cabot Cove Inn." The inn, and the town, were used as a location for "Cabot Cove" in the old *Murder, She Wrote* television series. The room is big enough for all of us, but when I see that the closets contain His and Hers terrycloth robes, I get in a romantic mood and rent the room next door for the kids. We kick 'em out of our room.

Dinner is at a "locals" restaurant, where we chat about the surrounding area. I ask if it's safe to take my Suburban and or motorcycle out Navarro Ridge Road, an isolated dirt road that goes deep into the backcountry.

"Oh, sure."

"What about … farmers?" It is well known that the Northern California area is a marijuana growing area.

"Well," comes the reply, "you don't want to go off the main dirt road. But you should be safe if you stick to the main route."

"Should be safe" isn't quite good enough for me, and the next day we stay on Highway One and head further up the coast.

Highway One pulls away from the coast just past Rockport and heads inland. There starts the "Lost Coast," a 70 mile stretch with no coast highway and little development. It is the most isolated and undeveloped section of coastal California. There is a dirt road that goes through the area, and we love the idea of exploring the Lost Coast in our four wheel drive Suburban. But, we're going to stick to the main dirt road.

I unload the motorcycle and give my children turns riding on back while Katie drives the Suburban. The road is quite rutted and bumpy, and there are numerous places where the Suburban has to crawl through. Even then, Katie and the kids get jounced pretty hard against the shoulder straps. Late in the afternoon when we again reach paved road, I put the motorcycle back onto the Suburban and we drive into Shelter Cove.

Shelter Cove is a planned community in the middle of the Lost Coast. In the center of the community is an airstrip surrounded by a golf course. The idea is for wealthy Bay Area residents to be able to fly in and stay at their weekend homes there. It is a rugged, desolate, and beautiful part of the world. Shelter Cove itself is a headland that shelters a small bay from the northern swell. The fishing is said to be excellent.

We get a room at the Shelter Cove Motor Inn, right on the water, overlooking the rocks and tide pools. Two rooms on the beach cost a little less than I usually pay for one room.

During the night, a ferocious thunderstorm comes up. The waves crash against the rocks and the lightning flashes, catching the sea spray in mid arc, the fury of nature seized in the act. The noise is tremendous.

The next morning Katie emerges from the bathroom in a terrycloth bathrobe, and with an odd expression on her face. I ask her what is wrong. She tells me she has found a lump in her breast. She touches awkwardly just inside her robe, near the top of her right breast. She places my hand about two or three inches below her collarbone. The lump is very prominent and easy to feel. I ask her what she wants to do. She says nothing. Then she says she'll continue to check it. It's sore. She thinks it's a bruise from the seatbelt shoulder strap smacking into her on the bumpy dirt roads of the "Lost Coast."

We make a leisurely drive into Trinidad, arriving late in the afternoon.

Trinidad, like Shelter Cove, is a sheltering headland. It is near the highway and more populous, but still rather remote. It is a beautiful place where the forest steps down the boulders almost to the sea.

Our friends, the O'Brien's, live in Trinidad in a large home on seven acres, and have invited us to stay with them.

Most days I escape from Trinidad where it is sixty degrees and foggy, and drive inland to Willow Creek, where the air is ninety degrees and the river is sixty, clear, and invigorating. I swim and fish and in my fishing, thankfully catch nothing but sunlight. I love to be in and along rivers during the heat of the summer. The river washes my cares away.

During our stay in Trinidad, the burdens of twenty years of corporate life, and of anxiously seeking to make a living each day, fall off like scales. I am surprised that it has taken all these months to happen, but am delighted that it is now happening. For the first time in my adult life, I'm (mostly) living the advice of Luke 12:22-31, a passage that I have long known and, to varying effect, often recited to myself:

> *Then Jesus said to his disciples, "Therefore I tell you, do not worry about your life, what you will eat; or about your body, what you will wear. Life is more than food, and the body more than clothes. Consider the ravens: They do not sow or reap, they have no storeroom or barn; yet God feeds them. And how much more valuable you are than birds! Who of you by worrying can add a single hour to his life? Since you cannot do this very little thing, why do you worry about the rest?*

"Consider how the lilies grow. They do not labor or spin. Yet I tell you, not even Solomon in all his splendor was dressed like one of these. If that is how God clothes the grass of the field, which is here today, and tomorrow is thrown into the fire, how much more will he clothe you, O you of little faith! And do not set your heart on what you will eat or drink; do not worry about it. For the pagan world runs after all such things, and your Father knows that you need them. But seek his kingdom, and these things will be given to you as well."

I look up my old notes from January. The time has not been wasted. I wrote:

"Today I will appreciate all the blessings God has given me. I also promise myself not to try to figure out how I will wring even more blessings out of Him in some future day. If I don't climb completely off the hamster wheel, I will have wasted this precious gift of time. Instead, I want to always look back on this time as a turning point, a lightening of the load."

I confess that this "sabbatical" was not only to spend time with my kids. More than anyone, it was to spend time with my self.

When I look in the mirror, I see my self, I recognize my self completely. My eyes are relaxed and at peace, and I can easily see and recognize the person they reflect. Gone is the twitch in my right eye from corporate days, and welling up, from deep inside, is sweet ambition. Not the soured ambition of "should," or "ought to," but the ambition of creativity, energy, a yearning to collaborate with the gifts my Maker gave me, a giving back to God. I am filled with a joy that emanates from deep within my core, within the giving, unique, creating seed God planted in me.

I'm ready. I can't wait to get home, unpack, and finish the summer with my wife and kids, then send the kids off to school on the Tuesday after Labor Day.

Then, I'll create something amazing in this world.

We say goodbye to the O'Brien's, to Trinidad, and head home.

Katie has to get that lump checked out. The soreness has gone away and it must be some kind of cyst or bruise inside. I'm not worried. She's not worried. She had that mammogram at the end of June, and it was completely clear.

Katie wants to start oil painting. Vanessa is going to be starting Kindergarten. Shawn will start 3rd grade, Alex will start Junior High and Michael will start High School.

Even though we are in the very middle of raising our children, there will be time for just the two of us when they are in school. Katie and I haven't had that kind of time since Mikey was born, and a lot of parents *never* have that. We are truly blessed.

When we get home, one of the first things I do—even before we're done unpacking the Suburban—is dig my watch out of the back of the drawer and put it back on.

✳✳✳✳✳

When Mikey was about six, I taught him to use my BB gun rifle. Some people might think that's too early, but I felt that, like it or not, we live in a bit of a gun culture. Better to teach him how to handle a gun safely when he's young and to learn a healthy respect, even fear, for the damage and destruction guns can cause.

So, on many afternoons back then, I knelt next to my little boy in the side yard, taking him step-by-step through The Eight Steps of Safe BB Gun Firing.

Before we could start, of course, he had to have a target area that would be safe and not cause the BB to ricochet. We stacked some hay bales and in the middle of the stack, posted a paper bull's-eye. We placed a broomstick about fifteen feet back from the target. This would be our firing line.

Next, of course, my son had to have protective eyewear. Not just any protective eyewear, but something that would keep a BB from coming in the side, top, or front. We used ski goggles with clear, shatterproof polycarbonate lenses. They were Junior-sized, so that the strap could be adjusted to keep them properly snug on his precious little head.

I wrote out the Eight Steps of Safe BB Gun Firing on a card, with Explanations, and insisted that he memorize The Eight Steps, and understand the Explanations completely:

THE EIGHT STEPS OF SAFE BB GUN FIRING
(WITH EXPLANATIONS)

1) SAFETY ON: Son, the safety always goes on first. Before you ever pick up a gun or are handed a gun, make sure the safety is ON.

2) PUMP: Now that the safety is on, pump the lever on the BB gun three times. One, two, three.

3) LOAD: Yes son, you may now carefully load one (1) BB into the gun.

4) SHOULDER: Raise the gun up and settle it in to your shoulder, pointing the barrel toward the bull's-eye. Your fingers stay away from the trigger area during this step.

5) SAFETY OFF: After the gun is in control and pointing toward the bull's-eye, you gently click the safety off.

6) AIM: Relax into a steady firing position. All focus is on the bull's-eye. If you are distracted for any reason, immediately click the safety ON before moving your eyes off the target. Now, gently bring your finger onto the trigger. Take final aim, and when ready...

7) FIRE: Gently squeeze the trigger while holding perfectly still.

8) SAFETY ON: That's right, son. Do not forget, you are not finished until you put the safety back ON.

Michael learned well, operated the gun very conscientiously, and became a pretty good shot. After a few months I allowed him to shoot the BB gun on his own. Of course, he had to ask permission first, then I would take the gun out from its secret hiding place and make sure he had his goggles on.

I would watch my little boy out in the side yard yell out, "SAFETY ON!" (I required him to bark out each of The Eight Steps of Safe BB Gun Firing, in order, loud enough for me to hear. If he didn't, he knew the gun would go bye-bye.) "PUMP! LOAD! SHOULDER! SAFETY OFF! AIM! FIRE! SAFETY ON!"

About that time, when Mikey was six and Alex was about four, Alex stood outside one day throwing darts into the wall of the house. He had six or eight darts and would throw them at the house, where they would chink off a flake of stucco and fall to the ground or, occasionally, stick in. He would then walk over, examine how each of them landed, retrieve them and return to his launching point to throw them again.

One day when Alex was doing this, Mikey needed to walk past Alex. "Alex," he said, "I'm coming through, okay? Alex? Ceasefire, all right? Alex? Alex?" Mikey said as he made his way past Alex. Just as he was passing, out of the corner of his eye, he saw Alex's arm swing rapidly down. Incredulous, Mikey turned to yell at Alex, and at that moment the point of the dart sunk into Mikey's cheek, just below the left eyeball.

Alex screamed in terror and ran into the house while Mikey stood, stunned. Alex ran to Katie and screamed that he had "poked Mikey's eye out with a dart." Katie ran outside to find Mikey still standing there, slowly, sadly shaking his head as the dart swung and dangled from his face like a picador's lance. A drop of blood ran down his cheek, mixing with tears. She carefully pulled it out and a spurt of blood shot out onto her blouse. Alex watched it all in horror while hiding behind her. When he saw the blood, he started to retch.

She told him to run inside the house and get a paper towel, but Alex clung to her leg and screamed, "He's going to *kill* me! He's going to *kill* me!"

"No, Alex, he's not going to kill you."

"Yes, he is!" Alex retorted.

"Yes, I am!" Mikey shouted.

"Just go get the towel," she said. Alex released his grip and sped into the house.

Mikey moaned, "I can't believe it! He threw a dart in my eye!"

"No, honey, it's not in your eye, it didn't go in your eye."

"I can't believe he did it! He's so *stupid!*"

"We don't say, 'stupid' honey."

"But he is!"

Silence from Katie, because she secretly, wholeheartedly, emphatically agreed.

The blood was cleaned up and the darts put away on a high shelf in Daddy's workshop that day, to be taken down only by Daddy and used under one hundred percent supervision. The darts are still there.

When Alex got to be about six, he did receive some BB gun training from me, I think. Son Number Two. As I recall, by the time I showed him, it was obvious to me that he was already pretty handy with a firearm.

When Shawn, Son Number Three, was about five, I came home one day to find him standing in the side yard shooting the BB gun—a pair of sunglasses at his feet— reciting, "PUMP, LOAD, FIRE! PUMP, LOAD, FIRE! PUMP, LOAD, FIRE!" and shooting at a stack of rocks by the fence.

I politely took the gun away from him, explaining that I have to put it away until I had time to show him The Eight Steps of Safe BB Gun Firing.

In the late part of summer vacation, life around the house always becomes perilously dull. Boys, who will be boys, run out of things to do and loudly announce that they are "bored." Parents can't wait for school to start.

Advice to parents: That, "I'm bored" phrase, coming from a boy, late in the summer, is a warning. I strongly recommend immediately finding something safe for them to do, or it will mean a trip to the Emergency Room. Ever notice how many kids are wearing a cast on the first day of school?

This day, they give us fair warning. They say, "I'm bored, Dad, I'm bored," and I, not following my own advice, say, "Go find something to do."

This leaves them to act upon the ideas of their own perilous, hazardous imaginations...

I walk into our kitchen. It's a hot, late afternoon. The door into the back yard is wide open. I am standing there not doing anything in particular when I hear a dull "poof!" sound, followed by a distinct metallic "tic!" sound. A BB bounces into the house, rolls across the wooden floor and comes to rest against the far wall.

"Good one!" I hear one of the boys cry from outside. "That's a double!"

"Wheredit go?" another asks.

"*Its-in-the-house-I'll-get-it.*" Michael walks into the house and begins searching around on the floor for the BB, then to me: "Dad, have you seen a BB?"

"Yeah, one just rolled by. It's over there," I say, and point it out.

"Thanks," he says, and goes to retrieve it. On the way out the door he calls to his brothers, "Who's up next?"

Finally, my parental instincts awaken. I run outside. "What are you guys doing?"

Shawn is standing near the house, pumping the BB gun, the barrel waving wildly about at every thing and every one. "I hope that's not loaded yet," I say, sternly.

"No Dad, it's not loaded," he says, "I know about The Three Steps: PUMP! LOAD! FIRE!"

"What are you guys doing?" I ask again.

"Baseball," Mikey says, and indicates Alex, who is standing near the back fence. I squint to look at Alex. It takes me a while to register what I see: Alex is standing near the back fence wearing nothing but shorts. His big brown eyes are steadily focused beyond me, toward Shawn. He brings the metal bat up into position and readies his batting stance.

POOF! The BB gun fires and Alex takes a swing.

"Strike!" Mikey calls.

"STOP!" I yell, "What are you guys doing?"

"I told you, Dad. Baseball. BB Gun Baseball."

"Wait a minute," I say.

Shawn starts pumping the gun again.

"Stop! Shawn! Stop! Put the safety on!"

"What's a safety?" he asks.

244

"Safety. It's this button over here." I walk over and click it on. "Give me the gun."

"Why?"

"Give … me … the … gun."

"Okay," he says, agreeably, and hands it to me, the barrel jabbing up under my chin.

"Shawn, there are not Three Steps, there are Eight. The Eight Steps of Safe BB Gun Firing. Do you know them?"

"Uhm … Shoot, Skin, Cook, Eat…?"

"Boys, Line Up." When I need to communicate to the kids, I say, "Line Up." The youngest stands in front, the oldest in back, all facing me so that I can see them all at once and talk to them, (okay, lecture them) all at once.

"Boys," I say, "you cannot play BB Gun Baseball."

"*Why-not?*" Mikey whines.

"Gosh," I say, "where do I start? Uhm … Mikey, do you remember when Alex threw the dart and it went in your eye?" Alex looks at the ground.

Mikey says, "It didn't go in my eye."

"Well, you know what I mean."

"Okay." He knows what I mean.

"We could wear goggles," Shawn offers.

"No. No goggles. This is why, boys. Don't you understand what could *happen*?" Then with great drama, lowering my voice and speaking slowly, weightily, I say, "Somebody could get *shot*." I pause to let the silence surrounding that word "shot" sink in. I search each boy's face to assure myself that they all understand the gravity of "shot." I slowly shake my head in a scolding way, impressing on them the finality of it if, heaven forbid, somebody should get *shot*. By this time, they've broken out of formation in an effort to diffuse my glare.

There is a long silence. Then Mikey quickly mutters, *"Doesn't-really-hurt-that-bad."*

"WHAT?" I turn to him, incredulous.

"Nothing."

"What did you say?"

"Doesn't really hurt that bad," he enunciates.

From behind me, one of the boys mutters, "Then why did you shoot me *back?*"

"Well, *you* shot *me!*" Mikey retorts over my shoulder.

"It was an accident, but *YOU* did it on purpose, Mikey."

"Stop, stop, wait a minute, boys."

Shawn the peacemaker steps forward and, with big earnest eyes, says, "Really Dad, don't worry, it doesn't hurt that bad."

"Hold everything. Boys. Stop. Line up." I hold the gun far away from them. "Who here has NOT been shot by their brother? Raise your hand."

There is a long silence, a shuffling of feet, the conspiratorial shooting of secret looks at one another.

Nobody's hand goes up.

"Okay, guys, this gun is history. Nobody is going to use this gun any more. Say bye-bye to this gun." The BB gun is going to stay locked up. Well, at least until next summer.

All of this inspires me to leave you with An Final Poeym:

JOHN VALDEZ

AN POEYM,
By John Valdez
"Boys Will BB Boys"

My boys are now a bigger size
My boys, at last, are now more wise
No longer throwing darts in eyes.

My boys discovered this was fun:
Baseball with a BB gun
Much safer in comparison

My boys are victims, one, two, three
Of BB gun insanity
From brothers on a shooting spree

Oh, Alex, Shawn and Mikey are
The upid-stest of kids, by far
(We don't say stupid. But they are.)

My boys will grow and move away
To raise their own small boys some day
I hope they join the NRA.

'Cause when boys grow, they're great big boys
And all that changes is their toys
And fps, and muzzle noise.

*****

Friday.

We are at Dr. Russell's office, Katie's OB/GYN. He examines her, he checks the mammogram from June. There is nothing on the mammogram. She tells him about the Suburban bouncing down the dirt road to Shelter Cove, and how she found the lump the next day where the shoulder strap had smacked into her. Her story convinces me that it's a bruise, but it doesn't convince Dr. Russell.

He shakes his head, "It's probably not a hematoma, or you would have had some visible bruising. This has to be a cyst. We'll just drain it and you'll be fine."

Katie asks if it could be cancer, and he laughs.

"It can't be cancer. First of all, most of the time these lumps are not cancer. But more importantly, though cancer cells *do* grow quickly, even *they* cannot divide as quickly as this. You had this mammogram in June and it was clear, right?"

"Right."

He shakes his head. "Then it's not cancer. It would take at least a couple of years for cancer to grow to the size I feel here—it's about three or four centimeters across. Something would have shown up on the mammogram. But a cyst can grow just like that." He snaps his fingers. We feel total relief.

We ask him to drain the cyst right away, but he explains that, "There is a protocol. We need another mammogram first. It's just a formality. We are required to verify the diagnosis of any breast mass before doing any procedure. That's just policy."

He gives us lab orders and we head off down the hall for another mammogram, smiling and holding hands. It's late in the day and we won't have results 'til Monday.

Monday morning.

We get a call from Dr. Russell's office. He would like us to make an appointment with Dr. Michelle Alexander, a surgeon. It isn't a cyst, it's some kind of a mass. We get him on the phone. When we ask, he repeats that, in his opinion, cancer cannot grow this quickly, but that we really need to consult with Dr. Alexander.

Thursday.

4:27 p.m. Dr. Alexander's secretary squeezed us in. I look around the examination room. Box of napkins. Box of rubber gloves. Rubber hammer. Click. Make that 4:28. I wonder if they validate parking. Silence. I smile at Katie, trying to reassure her. "Traffic's gonna be bad," I say. She smiles back, pained, looks away. Sun streams in between the shutters. "Shall I open them?" I ask. She shakes her head.

Dr. Alexander bursts into the room. She is vivacious and drop-dead beautiful. She smiles and the room lights up, and so do we. Clutching Katie's medical chart, she introduces herself and shakes our hands. She is beaming. I feel better already.

Dr. Alexander examines Katie and looks at the new mammogram. "This looks like cancer to me," is her opener, smiling.

I chuckle, and start in, trying to quote Dr. Russell, only I am being a little condescending. "It's obviously *not* cancer, Dr. Alexander, because, as you no doubt know, cancer cannot grow this fast. Her June mammogram, as you see there, was clear."

"I don't like the way this looks at all…" she continues, still smiling, ignoring me.

"Cancer cells can't divide that fast, Dr. Alexander. Right?" I decide I don't like her.

She continues to ignore me. "This needs to come out, but I have to get a needle biopsy first to see what we are dealing with." She lowers Katie back onto the examination table, opens the door, and calls for her assistant.

"Dr. Alexander, wait," I say. "This is going too fast. We need to talk." She has said, "cancer" and "I don't like this" and "biopsy" in the first ten seconds, words Katie and I have successfully avoided for an entire month.

Alexander stops and looks at me.

"Dr. Alexander, I don't want her to have a needle biopsy!"

"Why not?"

"Because, if it IS cancer—which it can't be—and it's encapsulated, I don't want you to pop it open and turn cancer loose into her system."

"Listen," she says, "all the studies show there is no difference in survivability when a needle biopsy is done first."

Great. Here are more words to hate: "Survivability." "Studies show…" isn't far behind.

I think of Katie's mother, Margaret. Her tumor was encapsulated, too, except for the hole made in it by the biopsy.

She says, "I need to know what is going on in there before we operate." The nurse enters the room with a tray that has a large needle on it. I can't breathe.

I say, "Despite the 'studies', don't you think it's intuitively obvious that if you have cancer and it's encapsulated, that it's a bad idea to literally pop open that Pandora's box? I don't want to unleash whatever is in there into Katie's system!"

"Look at this latest mammogram," she says, "besides clearly showing the tumor, you can see where it's sending out these tendrils, here, here, and here, into the surrounding tissue. If this is cancer—and it sure looks to me like it is—then the 'Pandora's box,' as you call it, is already open. This cancer is unencapsulated. It's in her system, hon. She's Stage II/Stage III. It's 3 or 4 centimeters across and has to be at least a year old."

"*If* it's cancer."

"That's right. Now I need to know what we are dealing with before we go to surgery."

I put my face in my hands. "How soon can we have surgery?"

"Two and a half weeks," the nurse interjects, lowering Katie flat on her back on the table. "Now honey," she says to Katie, "I just need you to relax."

"Wait a minute," I say. "Why do we have to wait two and a half weeks? If this thing has grown this big since June and is sending out 'tendrils' and is into her system, why on earth don't we do surgery the day your biopsy results come back?"

"Well, the studies show there is no difference in long term survivability if the tumor is removed within two months. Some studies show you can wait as long as six months."

Now I officially hate the phrase, "studies show..." This is the most unbelievable nonsense I have ever heard in my life. Study, shmuddy. An expletive erupts from me, loudly, which refers to what comes out of the back end of a boy cow. How can they sit there straight-faced and feed me this? I feel a dark cloud of anger well up all the way from my toenails.

"I don't care about the studies. This is not a study, this is my wife. You said this is at least a year old, and yet look at the June mammogram and tell me where the tumor is."

"I'm not a radiologist."

"Oh, please give me a break. Look at the mammogram."

She looks, then says, "That's not the mammogram we need to worry about. We need to worry about the latest one."

"If this is cancer," I continue, "you've never seen it grow this quickly before, have you?"

I get non-committal looks at the floor. After a long silence, Dr. Alexander says, "This *is* unusual."

"Then don't tell me about 'studies.' Will you try to get an earlier surgery date?"

"Yes." She turns to the nurse. "Karen, will you work on that?" Karen nods and leaves the room.

"Katie and I need to talk," I say. "Would you excuse us? Katie, would you please sit up? I don't want to be making decisions while we are flat on our back."

When Alexander leaves I say, "I don't like this lady."

"I think she's right, John."

"I think she's ... I think she may be right, too, but ... do you want to get a second opinion?"

"That will take time. If it's cancer, I don't want to lose the time. The next guy is just going to want to do a biopsy, too, and then we will have lost that much more time. I just want to get this done. I want to get it over with."

"Do you trust her?"

"Yes."

I can't breathe. I can't talk. Finally, I am able to push out the words, "Do you trust her with your life?"

"I can't answer that, I don't know, I think so, I think I do."

"Let's pray. We have to pray."

We pray. We pray for peace, we pray for wisdom, we pray to ask God if we should trust Katie's life with this pushy lady whom we have known for five minutes.

When we stop praying, we come up, look at each other and say, "Okay. Let's do it."

We open the door to signal that we're ready for them. The nurse and Dr. Alexander come back in. The nurse says, "We may be able to get an earlier surgery date. I have someone working on it now."

"Thank you," I say. I never could have imagined that the best thing about the entire day was hearing that my wife might be able to have a chunk of her breast removed, sooner rather than later. By someone I do not like.

"When do we get our biopsy results back?"

"Monday."

"But Monday is Labor Day," someone says.

"Oh, that's right, let's see." The nurse looks at the calendar, "Yes, we'll get results on … gosh August went by fast…"

Then Dr. Alexander says, flatly, "Tuesday. The day after Labor Day."

"Tuesday?"

"Tuesday."

ABOUT THE AUTHOR

John Valdez lives and writes in Leucadia, California.
He is not related to Juan Valdez of Colombian coffee fame.

S.D.G.

71729184R00165

Made in the USA
Columbia, SC
03 June 2017